All The Right Moves

All The Right Moves

A Financial Road Map for the College Senior and New Graduate

by

Zachary D. Grossman

and

Janis Gade Landis

with their daughters
Joanna, Karen, and Jessica

Writers Club Press
New York San Jose Lincoln Shanghai

All The Right Moves
A Financial Road Map for the College Senior and New Graduate
Copyright © 2000 by Zachary D. Grossman and Janis G. Landis

ISBN: 0-595-00109-2

Published by Writers Club Press, an imprint of iUniverse.com, Inc.

For information address:
iUniverse.com, Inc.
620 North 48th Street
Suite 201
Lincoln, NE 68504-3467
www.iuniverse.com

URL: http://www.writersclub.com

Dedication

The authors dedicate this book to their families

and to the memory of

Susan Gade Grossman, 1942–1983.

Table of Contents

Acknowledgment

The authors gratefully acknowledge the expert assistance of Melanie Hurwitz, C.P.A. (Lebson and Associates, Baltimore, Maryland) who reviewed the entire manuscript for accuracy and made invaluable suggestions.

Introduction

"Why Should I Read This Book?" you ask.

We answer:

You've just graduated. You've got your first job. You've got a new place to live. If any of these apply to you, or soon will, then you have a long list of things to think about and do. And we strongly suspect that reading the fine print of checking account fees and stock market reports are not on that list.

WE DON'T BLAME YOU. They're not on our list either. We (Joanna, Karen, and Jessi) think money management is just about the dullest thing in the world. So we asked our parents to tell us the absolute minimum that we absolutely had to know, and then they (with our help) wrote that all down in this book.

And that's why this book is different—we know that you have better things to do, and if you had wanted to immerse yourself in money management, you would have majored in it. But, your folks want to be sure that you are taking care of your future, and you want to have enough to live well now. This book will show you the no-hassle, no-brainer way to accomplish these goals.

So here's our strategy:

We tell you the few simple things you need to know and do personally to get on the path to financial security down the road, including:

The disappearing pay check: When you receive your first pay check you find that you're taking home a lot less than you expected. This chapter explains where it all went (and how to get some of it back!).

We're not into bondage, and you don't have to be either: We guarantee that Part I of this chapter will tell you EVERYTHING you need to know (actually very little) about bonds, stocks, and investing.

We know that you plan to stay forever young, but just in case you retire someday, we introduce you to IRA, a very smart friend to have, who can do great things for you. But be warned—IRA works best with young people, so don't put him off.

Can you bank on your bank? Not all banks are created equal, and while cute ads may tempt, you'll find a smarter way to decide which account and which bank are best for you.

Sex and violence: Well, actually this chapter is about income taxes, but we figured if we said that you would have stopped reading. If you read tax publications for fun, skip this chapter, but if you're normal, we'll make paying taxes as painless as possible, while keeping you out of jail.

The backwards budget: Everybody keeps telling you that to save any money you need to set up a budget and live within it. But, who can live in anything that small? So we reverse the process, and start with the savings part—the only savings plan that works. And frankly, the reason why it works is that once set in motion it requires absolutely no will power or conscious act whatsoever on your part. If only a diet could be this easy!!

Credit cards: How to get the most out of these little devils without letting them take everything out of you.

Credit: Need a loan? Falling behind on payments? How to get the credit you need without being discredited.

Student Loans: How to pay back what you owe, understand what you're doing, and avoid default in tough times.

Putting it all together: When you've read this far into the book, and followed the few (and we mean few) simple steps we've shown you, you'll have a plan that even your genius cousin, the financial whiz, can't beat. You will have established your own personal long-term money management plan that will go on working for you and you won't ever have to worry about it again. Your personnel office, bank, and other folks (who, after all, must like this kind of thing or otherwise they wouldn't be in the business) will worry about it for you.

Read and reap…

Chapter 1

Your First Check Stub:
What it Tells You and What it Doesn't

The good news is: you're on your own; the bad news is: **you're on your own!** TGIP (Thank God It's Payday!). But hold it—hold on a minute—somebody goofed—*somebody must have*—the pay for your seven-dollar-an-hour job, worked 40 hours last week, isn't $280. It's less—*a lot less*. What's all that mumbo-jumbo on the paper stuck to the check? How about taxes? Will "the government" want even more later? Maybe the "parental dole" wasn't so bad after all…

Where oh where has the little pay gone? "Gross" and Net":

"Gross pay" is what you earn before anyone takes anything out.

"Net pay" is what you have left after taxes (federal, state, and local), union dues (if any), health insurance, pension plans, charities, etc. swallow up their share. "Net pay" is the same as take-home pay.

So how does it work?

An employer is required by law to deduct tax from your paycheck and send it to the government before paying you—this tax withheld is called "withholding" and includes U.S. Government (Federal) tax and, in many states, State Income Tax. (A few cities also have a City Income Tax). The percentage of your income deducted for Federal and State Income Tax depends upon your earnings: **the more you earn, the greater the percentage you pay.** (This principle—higher earners pay a higher percentage—is called a *"graduated income tax"* and is considered fair or unfair depending upon your perspective, but it has been tax policy in most industrialized nations for nearly a century).

Attached to each paycheck is a sheet called a "stub" that explains what you have been paid for a "pay period"—usually a week or two. At a minimum, the stub indicates the gross amount you earned during that pay period, what was taken out, and what you received (the "net"). Many stubs also indicate the amount taken out for a particular purpose so far during the current year. ("YTD" or "year-to-date".)

An entry-level clerk—I. Will Struggleon:

I. Will Struggleon, unmarried, childless entry-level file clerk, works 40 hours a week, at $5.20/hour, for Paypoor Inc. (New York City office); gross weekly pay (before anyone takes anything out) is $ 208, and yearly gross pay is $10,816. Take a look at Will's weekly stub, calculated for a typical recent tax year—each year is a little different.

I. Will Struggleon CHECK DATE 6/29/__			
Employee's Statement of Salary and Deductions			
Social Security No. 000-000-000	Gross Pay 208.	Net Pay 172.24	
Soc. Sec. Tax 12.72	Federal Tax 15.90	State Tax 2.18	City Tax 1.95
Fed. Ex 1	State Ex. 1	Medicare Tax 3.01	

"Federal Tax" is the amount taken out for United States Government Income Tax.

"State Tax" is the amount deducted for the state in which you work.

I. Will Struggleon is paid by the hour, so the stub will also include an hourly rate and the number of hours worked:

Pay period: 1/7/__ to 1/14/__

Rate (the amount Will earns per hour) **Hours** (the number of hours Will worked) **Amount**
5.25   40   208

You must be kidding! Does a working stiff like Will Struggleon really have to pay all this tax? I thought folks like me—I mean like Will—get a break!!

Yes and No. Enter the "Exemption":

Mercifully, the Federal government leaves a portion exempt from taxes, $2650 (in a recent typical tax year), for the wage earner and an equal amount for each "dependent", that is, each person whose support depends upon the wage earner. So, if Will Struggleon is a single wage earner with no children, taxable income becomes $10,816 minus $2650, or $8166. In tax jargon, Will has "*claimed one exemption.*" If there is a "dependent spouse"—that is, a non-working spouse whose support depends upon Will—taxable income drops another $2650 to $5616 ("*claimed two exemptions*"). If they have a dependent child, taxable income drops yet another $2650 to $3066 ("claimed three exemptions.") Obviously, even a few exemptions at a low income level reduces taxable income a lot, but the exemption of $2650 per wage earner and per dependent is the same for higher earners.

So why not claim oodles of exemptions (like eight non-existent kids) and have virtually no tax withheld?

GOOD QUESTION!!

ANSWER: Because at the end of the "tax year" (April 15,) when you submit your official tax form (called "filing your tax return") to Uncle Sam, you would have to either lie about the non-existent exemptions (a Federal Crime) or pay back all of the money that should have been withheld, along with interest and possibly penalties!! BUT—claiming less than your true number of exemptions can be cool, as we will soon see.

On your stub:

"Fed. Ex." indicates the number of exemptions you have claimed for purposes of determining your withholding for Federal Tax.

"State Ex." indicates the number of exemptions you have claimed for purposes of determining your withholding for State Tax. (Believe it or not, you can "claim" different numbers of exemptions for federal and state tax! It is not improper, for example, to set your state tax withholding at "one person, single" while on your federal withholding you claim "zero" (so as to have more money withheld for federal tax.)

"Fed. Ex." and "State Ex." are pretty obvious abbreviations, but some stubs put it another way:

Tax Filing Status
       Federal   S 01

       State   S 01

"S" indicates single; "M" would indicate married. (This information counts, because the tax rates for single and married people may differ.) The "01" on the "Federal" line means one federal exemption, and the "01" on the "State" line means one State exemption.

O.K., O.K., I get it, but why would anyone want to have more tax dollars withheld from their paycheck then they have to?

When you start working, you are asked to fill out a basic form called a "W-4" that asks how many exemptions you claim; this information allows your employer to calculate how much tax to withhold from your paycheck. The fewer the exemptions you claim, the higher your taxable income will appear, and the more tax will be deducted from your check. Legally, you can claim the number of exemptions you really have, **or you can claim fewer exemptions—even zero exemptions.** In other words, you can be married with a dependent spouse and two dependent children (four exemptions—yourself, your spouse, and two kids) and claim no exemptions; a lot of tax would be deducted and withheld from your check, so your take home pay will be less, but you would receive a full refund (admittedly without interest) of the overpayment soon after you send in your tax form (CHAPTER 5). **This refund can be a key element of your savings plan** (CHAPTER 10). But, if you claim too many dependents, you may owe tax, an unhappy prospect.

Other stuff on just about everybody's stub:

Social Security Tax (Soc. Sec. Tax): *Earned income up to about $68,400 is taxed at 6.2%* to pay for your government retirement plan (Social Security).**Don't be fooled-you will need other retirement plans (CHAPTER 3) to ensure a comfortable old age.** ."Social Security Tax" is sometimes abbreviated "F.I.C.A." (Federal Insurance Contribution Act) or O.A.S.D.I. (Old Age Survivors and Disabilities Act).

Medicare Tax: *All earned income, with no ceiling, is taxed at 1.45% to pay for Medicare, the government health insurance plan for persons over 65 (and, in some special cases, younger persons).*

Had just about enough? Hang on for another minute or two—we're almost through the boring stuff. **Skip to** *Miscellaneous other deductions—the "code"* (unless you're interested in what happens when you earn a lot more.).

A More Complicated Stub at the Higher End: Successful Pediatrician—Dr. Richard Thanyou:

Richard Thanyou, M.D., Syracuse, New York H.M.O. pediatrician, works 44 hours a week, at an annual salary of $73,397 (weekly gross pay of $1411.48). But the doctor's take-home pay will be much less, $823.04. Dr. Thanyou's gross pay is much greater than Will Struggleon's, but take home pay is proportionally smaller; in other words, *the percentage* of the doctor's income paid in taxes is much higher. Thanyou's take home pay is also lowered by health insurance premiums, charitable contributions, a court-ordered child support withhold, and pension deductions. (Mercifully, Syracuse, New York has no city income tax).

Richard Thanyou   CHECK DATE: 6/29/__

Employee's Statement of Salary and Deductions

000-000-000 Social Security No.	**1411.48** Gross Pay	**823.04** Net Pay
86.37 Soc. Sec. Tax	**205.91** Federal Tax	**75.25** State Tax
2245.62 YTD Soc. Sec. Tax	**5353.66** YTD Federal Tax	**1956.50** YTD State Tax
37020.01 YTD. Gross Salary	**73397.00** Annual Pay	**Fed. Ex.** **State Ex.** 4 3
Medicare Tax 20.46		

Dr. Thanyou makes a good buck, so his weekly federal tax is high— $205.91.

"YTD Federal Tax" is the amount of United States Government Income Tax taken out so far—"year-to-date". By 6/29 Dr. Thanyou has had $6,182.77 deducted for the feds.

The doctor's weekly state tax is $75.25. State taxes vary enormously; some states have no state tax, while others tax up to 9%!! (The family often contemplates a move to Connecticut, where the good doctor will earn as much and pay far less in state tax). When you consider any job, its salary must be seen as gross income and also in terms of taxes you would pay in that state. Even if the state tax factor is insignificant, an inquiry will alert the employer to your financial savvy.

"YTD State Tax" is the amount of State Tax taken out so far this year.

Although the Thanyou family has four exemptions (two parents and two children), they would have to breed like rabbits to produce enough exemptions for a really major dent in their taxable gross income.

Miscellaneous other deductions—the "code":

Words like "gross pay" and "net pay" are short, but some items like "United Auto Workers Union dues", "donation to the United Way", or "company pension plan" are simply too long to fit into the limited space on a stub. So, stubs may have two or more columns called "other deductions", which often identify these items by "code". To increase the confusion, *"code" is a number and "amount" is a number!!*

CODE	AMOUNT	CODE	AMOUNT
650	20.46	195	76.00
138	101.21	270	2.78

On the back of the stub, in tiny print, each code is defined: for example, item 650 represents Dr. Thanyou's pension contribution, $20.46 per check. Item 138 represents a court mandated deduction for child support (child of a previous marriage), $101.21. Item 195 is the health insurance premium for the family, $76.00. Item 270 represents the Doctor's meager contribution to charity, $2.78 per check.

O.K. Now I know what my check stub tells me: what does it leave out?

Your check stub tells you exactly where each penny of your salary goes, but it doesn't tell you how to make the most of what you have left, and how to use the tax withholding mechanism to get into saving and investing. the next nine chapters do that.

Fasten your seatbelts…

(By the way, for purposes of explanation, the specific dollar figures used in this chapter refer to one typical tax year. The principles explained here remain constant, but because the tax code is updated yearly, you will need updated information before calculating your own tax for the current year. Don't even begin to worry about this until you've read through CHAPTER 5. It turns out that information is so readily available that updating the details is no sweat.)

Chapter 2

Stocks, Bonds, and Mutual Funds:
The Boring Stuff that Makes Rich People Rich

Part I: Give Us Twenty Minutes and We'll Give You All You Need to Know

Now that you see how the money in your check is spread around, we'll cover how to invest some of what remains. Happily, a little accurate investment knowledge is a very good thing, while greater knowledge can be dangerous, because people who know more about investing often try to "outsmart" the investment world and lose their shirts; intelligent beginners take good, tried-and-true advice, with excellent results. So, armed with only a few basic facts, you can maximize gains with minimal long-term risk.

Stocks: The Basics

When a privately-owned company decides to enlarge its ownership base—that is, give new people a chance to own a piece of the company—it issues shares of stock, each share representing an equal piece of the company. **A share of stock is worth what people will pay for it, no more and no less.**

A company "goes public"

Imagine a company making computer discs (call it Disco.), founded by the Nerd family, who built the business from a basement operation to a small factory employing 20. Wishing to expand, the company decides to "go public", issuing 200,000 shares of stock to the public at $10 per share. Disco. is known as a "comer" in the industry, and all shares are snapped up, raising $2,000,000, which Disco. designates for a factory expansion. (Aside from various brokerage fees and commissions, the money from this initial offering of shares goes to the company.) Of course, this maneuver dilutes company ownership—**each share holder now owns 1/200,000 of the company**, and, to keep effective control, the Nerd family arranges to buy a large block of Disco. stock.

After the initial sale, individuals "trade" shares, buying and selling to each other; the stock price stays around $10 per share. (None of the money paid for shares sold by one private party to another goes to the company.)

Problems and opportunity

Two weeks after Disco. "goes public" (the Initial Public Offering, or IPO), a fire sweeps through the Disco. plant. Alas, Papa Nerd—occupied with the stock issue and plans for expansion—failed to pay the company fire insurance premium! Panic spreads among shareholders, who assume that the company is in deep trouble. Immediately there are few buyers for Disco. shares. People trying to sell ("dump") their Disco. stock find it relatively worthless, because almost no one wants it. But some clever souls, who have researched the company carefully, know that the bricks and mortar of Disco.'s factory are of little importance to the company's long-term prospects, because Disco. holds patents on a superior manufacturing process. They buy "worthless" Disco. stock for $.50/share. Three years later, after a year of rebuilding and two years paying off a bank loan for reconstruction, Disco. is back in stride, making and selling discs by the ton; profits are pouring in, and there are buyers for the company's stock everywhere, with Disco. selling for $15/share. Previous buyers at the low of $.50/share now look very smart. The company feeds this rising stock price by paying out part of its profits to each shareholder in the form of a yearly dividend.

So what is a stock really worth?

Moral of this story: a stock is worth **only what people will pay for it, and that is determined by—and only by—supply and demand.** Lots of variables **should** factor into a stock's price, like the company's earnings, prospects for future earnings, value of its assets ("book value"), and dividends; sometimes these do, in fact, cause a rise or fall in a stock's price, but ultimately **the selling price of a stock is determined only by what buyers will pay.**

Buying and selling stock

Unlike used cars, jewelry, baseball cards, etc., stocks—often called "equities"— are sold almost exclusively through registered stockbrokers working through massive trading organizations called "stock exchanges." Two of the largest, the New York Stock Exchange and the American Stock Exchange, are physically located in New York; one can actually visit these hectic places and see hundreds of people in a state of seeming hysteria trading millions of shares each hour. (On a normal day, the New York Exchange handles the purchase and sale of

600,000,000 to 1,200,000,000 shares!) Individuals place orders to buy and sell through brokers, who pass the message to their "floor traders," who execute the trade. Contrary to popular belief, even on-line discount brokers use this mechanism, although the initial communication between customer and broker is via internet instead of by telephone. Another exchange, called the NASDAQ (National Association of Securities Dealers) trades mainly in cyberspace.

The Venerable "Dow Jones Industrial Average"

Clearly, on any day, some stocks rise (price goes up) and others fall (price goes down), but most Americans have heard—almost from infancy—that "the market was up today" or "the market was down", usually along with a number from the "Dow Jones Industrial Average." So what is this "Dow Jones Industrial Average" ("the Dow" or "DJIA" for short)? In the 1880's, when the New York Stock Exchange was young, investors had no way to measure market trends; a wild day on Wall Street simply could not be quantified, and a jumble of advances and declines in the value of stocks and bonds usually revealed no definable trend. On May 26, 1896, Charles H. Dow unveiled his Industrial Average of 12 stocks; if the average price of these representative industrial stocks rose, the "market" was up ("*bull market*"), and if they fell, the "market" was down ("*bear market*")(1). This elementary statistical device—primitive and obvious by today's standards—represented a major breakthrough in market quantification. The Dow has been repeatedly revised and expanded to include other key US corporations, like IBM, and now includes 30 companies (2). To account for complex maneuvers like stock "splits" (a company issues two shares for every one share held) the simple arithmetic average (total of 12 stock prices divided by 12) was altered, with a more complex divisor, **but the resulting number nonetheless continues to represent the average price of 30 major industrial stocks.** Other indexes—the Transportation Index and the Utilities Index—were added. Although partner Edward D. Jones did not contribute directly to the creation of the original index, it bears his name also. To this day, Dow Jones & Company owns and publishes The Wall Street Journal.

Other averages

The problem with the Dow and the other original indexes is that they represent only a tiny—although important—slice of the market, in which shares of thousands of companies are traded. To better represent the movement of shares of many large corporations, the Standard and Poor index of 500 major companies was created (the "S&P 500",) along with indexes representing smaller companies (the "Russell 2000" and the American Exchange "AMEX"). Of note, the NASDAQ average includes many small companies but is dominated by major technology giants, like Intel, Microsoft, and Cisco Systems, as well as key internet companies, like Yahoo and E-bay.

Bonds: The Basics

> The basic fact about bonds is that *a young investor has absolutely no need to know anything about them!!* This manual is to help you get started, not to waste your time. However, you will find some bond facts at the end of this chapter, under **Facts That Will Impress Your Parents.**

Mutual Funds: The Beginner's Key to Success

A stock mutual fund solicits money from individual investors, buys stocks, and manages them (trading) without consulting its investors; in other words, once investors choose a fund, they place their money in the hands of a professional manager and are relieved of the burden of selecting individual stocks and deciding if and when to trade. As stocks owned by the fund rise, the total worth of the fund rises, and the fund's shares increase in value (and vice versa!)

Funds operate according to publicly-listed guidelines, directing their investments to certain business sectors (like technology, precious metals, or agriculture), geographic locations (like China/Hong Kong, South America, Europe), or even philosophies ("contrarian"). All extract a yearly management fee, and **many levy a sales charge (called a "load")**, paid initially ("up front" or "front-end" load) or upon withdrawal of funds before a given period of time ("rear-end load"). **In general, funds with no sales charge ("no load") have performed as well as "load" funds. THE ONLY GOOD LOAD IS NO LOAD.**

For many years the number of available mutual funds was relatively small, so the choice of a fund to invest in was easier than the choice of a stock to buy; alas, in recent years the number of funds has ballooned hugely, and now the number of available funds approximately equals the number of individual stocks listed on the New York Stock Exchange!

Mutual fund "families," like Vanguard and Fidelity, manage a variety of different funds with varying approaches. Money can be switched from one fund to another, usually for a nominal transaction fee, over the phone. **These "families" usually also have a "money market mutual fund" that pays more interest than banks pay on a savings account;** you could get more than savings account interest yourself, at your local bank, by investing in a bank "certificate of deposit" (CD), but you are committed to leaving your money in the CD for a fixed period of time—usually at least six months—and banks assess a financial penalty for early withdrawal. In contrast, you can withdraw all or part of your money from a money market fund ("redeem shares") by phone, without penalty, within a few hours (although the check may arrive 3-4 days later, due to the speed of mail delivery).

In fairness, we admit that bank deposits are insured by a US Government Agency, the FDIC (Federal Deposit Insurance Corporation), so that even if your bank goes "belly up"—i.e., fails—you will get your money out safely, after some red tape. Money market funds, on the other hand, are not insured. Theoretically, if the investment company that manages your fund should collapse, your account could vanish. **However, to date no one has ever lost a penny in a US money market fund.** Your grandparents and some of your parents may harbor residual fears—left over from the Great Depression of the 1930's—of bank failures and life savings down the drain, and in fact, it is probably not prudent to keep your entire nest egg in a money market fund long term, but as a vehicle for parking cash on the way to bigger and better things, money market funds are ideal.

So mutual funds typically clobber the S&P 500, right?

Because all mutual funds have professional managers and research staffs ranging from a handful to hundreds, one would think that virtually any fund would be a **better** investment than the average of all stocks in the S&P 500, but, believe it or not, over the last thirty years **THE GREAT MAJORITY OF MUTUAL FUNDS HAVE UNDER PERFORMED THE S&P 500!!** In other words, 20 years ago, if you had bought one share of stock in each company that comprises the S&P 500, and held your shares passively, without any trading whatsoever, your stock collection ("portfolio") would be worth more than an equivalent investment in the vast majority of professionally-managed funds. Incredibly, the "no-brainer" method beats the "brainer" method almost every time!!

Enter the "Index Fund"

Unfortunately, buying one share of each stock in the S&P 500 or the Dow is impractical because of commissions charged; this problem has given rise to Index funds, which buy equal amounts of shares that make up one of the indexes, for example the S&P 500. **These funds are managed "passively,"** without trading once shares are purchased, and several are no load. By investing in an S&P 500 index fund you are guaranteed to equal the performance of the broad industrial market, year after year, outperforming the great bulk of mutual funds, unburdened by the need to pick and choose stocks on your own. **In the past 15 years, only 11 mutual funds have beaten the S&P 500 by more than 1.6% points per year, and several of these carry heavy loads, up to 6%!! (3). If a 15-year history is ancient for you, and you figure that "things must be different nowadays," digest this: The S&P 500 rose only 1.32% in 1994 but was up a whopping 37.58% in 1995 and 22.96% in 1996, beating 75% of ALL US STOCK FUNDS for 1994, 1995, and 1996 (4). It surged 33.36%, 28.58%, and 21.04% in 1997, 1998, and 1999.**

How To Read the Stock and Mutual Fund Pages:

Before surrendering our scarce dollars to the tender mercies of Wall Street, we must first confront and interpret its intimidating jargon, exemplified by the dreaded stock market and mutual funds pages of the Wall Street Journal. (Other newspapers use a similar, slightly less complex format.)

Examples:

January 14, New York Stock Exchange (affectionately called "**The Big Board**"—Dad will love that one).

52 weeks				Yield			Vol				
Hi	Lo	stock	sym	Div	%	PE	Vol	Hi	Lo	Close	Net Chg
29	22 1/2	IBP Inc.	IBP	.10	.4	8	1320	24 1/8	23 7/8	24	-1/8

First, note that Wall Street, which lives and dies by dollars and cents, currently uses whole numbers and fractions instead!! In other words, "22 1/2" means $22.50; "23 7/8" means $23.875. (This arcane system is inefficient, confusing, and therefore was considered permanent, until a recent rebellion in the ranks pushed through a change to decimals, effective mid 2000.) Second, the company name, under "stock", in this case, "IBP Inc.", which stands for Iowa Beef and Pork, Inc., may or may not be similar to the company's "symbol," abbreviated "sym". In fact, the "symbol" is of use only to professional brokers; you should look for your stock directly under the heading "stock", but you may have trouble finding it at first, because limited space usually requires abbreviation. Although Iowa Beef and Pork, Inc., is easily abbreviated "IBP", a stock like Countrywide Credit is abbreviated "CntrywdCd"; other abbreviations can be even more obscure. The "Hi and Lo" columns on the left, directly under "52 weeks," simply represent the highest and lowest prices the stock has sold for within the past 52 weeks, while the "Hi" and "Lo" columns to the right indicate the Hi and Lo for the day. **Most importantly: the number under "close" is the price at the end of the trading day, and the "net chg" is the increase or decrease in price** for that day. In our example, IBP closed at 24, with a loss of 1/8 per share—i.e., $ .125 for the day. For the time being, ignore all other columns and notations. (If you're particularly interested—see **Facts That Will Impress Your Parents.**)

The mutual fund tables, not as obscure:

Mutual Funds, January 14:

Name	NAV	Net Chg	YTD % ret
Jones	5.91	-0.01	+1.2

Mercifully, mutual funds list their value in conventional dollars and cents, rather than fractions; "5.91" means $5.91". "NAV" stands for "**Net Asset Value**"—i.e., **share price.** "Net Chg" indicates the gain or loss in value for the day—in this case, the Jones fund lost one cent. "YTD % ret" represents the year-to-date return in percent—i.e., the fund's increase in value or decrease in value for the calendar year thus far. Note that the Jones fund is up 1.2%, and the date is only January 14! In other words, an investment of $100 on January 1 would be worth $102 by January 14. (Not bad, considering that a bank savings account would probably give you 2 to 3 percent **for the entire year!**) If you think that is impressive, look at the Smith Group, "Global Technology B" (abbreviated "GlbTechB") on January, 27:

Name	NAV	Net Chg	YTD % ret
Smith Group GlbTechB	13.39	-0.17	+6.2%

Wow! In twenty-seven days, the share price of this fund has grown 6.2%!! Technology stocks, during January, are "hot."

Cool!! Let's buy low and sell high!!

Now, you say, why not move money into specific "hot" sectors as they go up, and take it out as they start to go down? Better yet, why not invest in an S&P 500 Index fund in a bull market, and pull out at the start of a bear market, only to buy in again when the market is low— i.e., buy low and sell high? This "strategy," a fantasy really, is called "market timing"—a sure way to stay poor, or if you are not poor, to become so. For the beginner—and probably for the experienced investor—timing the market is a fool's game. People who try to buy low and sell high, moving in and out of the market, often end up buying high and selling low. At your stage, never try to time the market. **Buy and hold, through good markets and bad. You are so young that your time horizon is very, very long, and if you don't put rent, grocery, or tuition money into the market, you can easily wait out any downturns.** (Incidentally, market downturns of 10% are euphemistically called "corrections.")

> **THE WAITING GAME BEATS THE CRYING GAME EVERY TIME.**

A Coherent Strategy for the Beginner:

You don't have much money. You don't have time to research individual stocks or mutual funds, and the chance of beating the S&P 500 with your own choices is low; the chance of beating the S&P 500 by a significant margin is very low, even for the seasoned professional. Stock brokers will flood you with advice, some of it good, on individual stocks and selected mutual funds, and in later years you may find yourself trading stocks or buying specific funds effectively and profitably, but for now, as a college student or new graduate, your strategies are clear:

(1) Buy a no load index fund that follows the S&P 500.

(2) Do not let anyone talk you into buying individual stocks *at this stage.*

(3) Do not—we repeat—do not attempt to "time" the market.

Whom to Call: Everybody wants to hear from you, so don't be shy.

Here are Consumer Report's top S&P 500 Index Funds—all no load, all with very low "expense ratios"—i.e., administrative overhead that is subtracted from share price (5).

Fund	Phone
BT Investment Equity 500 Index	1-800 730-1313
California Investment S&P 500 Index	" 225-8778
Dryfus S&P 500 Index	" 373-9387
T. Rowe Price Equity Index	" 638-5660
Vanguard Index 500	" 662-7447

ALAS, the minimum investment among these funds is $2500, so we run into the "minimum investment hurdle." Is there any way around this problem? YES!! Read on.

An Alternative Strategy:

There are plenty of slick mutual fund salespersons hungering for your dollars, all claiming that their fund beats the S&P 500 by a wide margin (we already know how likely that is!). However, a number of well-respected publications, notably Louis Rukeyser's Mutual Funds, Newsweek, Consumer Reports, and Morningstar, objectively and systematically rate mutual funds, both load and no-load. All of these rating systems involve long lists, time, concentration, and some degree of overchoice. As an alternative, we suggest the **TIAA-CREF Growth and Income Fund,** because: (1) Minimum investment is just $250, (2) the fund is no-load, (3) the fund's administrative overhead is among the lowest in the industry, and (4) about sixty percent of the fund's holdings are chosen to track the S&P 500, with the other 40 % actively managed. In other words, this fund offers a bit more risk along with a lot of attractive features.(6) TIAA-CREF can be reached at 1-800-223-1200. Incidentally, TIAA-CREF is a non-profit corporation with 80 years of money management experience.

Is there any other way to beat the minimum investment hurdle?

You bet!

(1) IN CHAPTER THREE WE CRASH THROUGH THIS PROBLEM: Uncle Sam to the rescue!!

(2) The Dow Diamonds and S&P 500 DR's

The What?

Until recently, S&P 500 Index Funds were believed to be the only available method of investing your money in such a way that it would increase or decrease in value along with the S&P 500 Index. And there was **no** way to invest in a vehicle whose value mirrored that of the mighty DOW. But, to the surprise of many professionals, a new investment vehicle called the "Dow Diamonds" appeared on 1/20/98. Quietly, with little fanfare, a similar product called "S&P 500 DR's" (S&P 500 Depository Receipts or SPDR's—pronounced "spiders") had appeared a few years earlier, virtually unnoticed by the Wall Street Pros.

The word "diamonds" in "Dow Diamonds" has nothing to do with gemstones; it simply refers to the cream of industrial companies that make up the DJIA—i.e., Wal Mart, Merck, IBM, etc.—the "diamonds" of American Industry. Similarly, "spiders" reflect the average share price of each company in the S&P 500. (The meaning of "DR" in "S&P 500 DR's" is so obscure that we won't waste your time with an explanation.)

Unlike mutual funds, that take your money and invest it in stocks, charging you administrative overhead and sometimes a load, with a high initial minimum investment, **the Dow Diamonds and S&P 500 DR's are bought and sold on the American Stock Exchange (AMEX) as stocks**; think of them as shares of a trust that holds Dow stocks or S&P

500 stocks as its assets. (The details of how the trust work are unimportant; **the key point is that you can buy as little as ONE SHARE of either trust, which is then guaranteed to move up or down with Dow or S&P 500 Index.**)

The price of a single "share" of the Dow Diamonds is set to be 1/100 of the DJIA, so if the DOW was at 9000, one share would cost you $90. If the DJIA rose to 10,000, your one share would rise to $100. Cool!!

O.K., with Dow Diamonds and "spiders" available, why bother with an S&P 500 Index Fund?

GOOD QUESTION!

Because buying stock always involves commissions, and shares of Diamonds and "spiders" are sold as stocks, so unless you use a DEEP DISCOUNT BROKER you would waste a couple of years' profits on purchase commissions. And, most stockbrokers, even deep discounters that execute trades by phone for only $15-$18 (by internet for $7.50 to $12), usually require a minimum initial balance in your account—about $1000. So we again run up against the "minimum investment hurdle," this time **not a minimum amount you must invest in any given fund or stock but the minimum you must deposit with a stockbroker to start an account!** (Note that National Discount Brokers—NDB.com on the Web—where you can open an account with **no minimum initial investment and no minimum monthly balance,** is a notable exception, but if your initial investment is small, say $250, the broker's commission of $14.75 for purchase of Diamonds or "spiders" comes to 5.9%—higher than almost any mutual fund load.) And, at National Discount Brokers, an IRA (next chapter) is subject to a $35 annual fee.

Nonetheless, we will keep the idea of Dow Diamonds and "spiders" alive as CHAPTER 3 vaults over the "minimum investment hurdle." For larger investments, the purchase of Diamonds or "spiders" makes good sense, because the commission charged for purchase of larger numbers of shares remains the same. Stay tuned.

Part II: Details, details, details—skip this part for the time being (or forever!) unless you have a particular interest in the subject—you already know everything you need to know to get started!!

Facts that will Impress Your Parents:

(1) The Composition of the Dow-Jones Industrial Average over the past century is a virtual time machine that mirrors the fortunes of industrial America (7).

> The original Dow included such now-extinct giants as American Cotton Oil, Distilling & Cattle Feeding Co., and U.S. Leather (a manufacturer of shoes, harnesses, saddles, and buggy whips!!). General Electric is the only member of the original 12 that remains in the current Dow. Other once-mighty companies, like Standard Rope and Twine, were included in 1896, only to be excluded later (1899). IBM was included in 1932, removed in 1939, and re-included in 1979! In 1998 WalMart replaced Woolworth's.

(2) Mutual Fund "philosophies" have gelled into basic categories, some of which include:

- "Balanced Funds" aim for a "balance" of stocks and bonds.

- "Equity Income Funds" invest in dividend-paying stocks.

● "Growth and Income Funds" pursue two objectives in choosing stocks: the potential for growth in share price and income from stock dividends.

● "Growth Funds" invest in rapidly-growing companies, whose stock hopefully will go up fast.

● "Aggressive Growth Funds" invest in stocks that hopefully will go up very fast.

● "Small Company Funds," as you might guess, invest in small, young companies with growth potential.

● "International Funds" invest in companies outside of the U.S.

● "Global Funds" invest in foreign and U.S. stocks.

● "Sector Funds" invest in companies of specific industries, like computers, biotechnology, food, transportation, or internet stocks.

● "Value Funds" buy up stock in great companies at bargain prices, when the companies are "out of favor on the street"—i.e., not pursued by Wall Street pros. Remember when Disco. was at $0.50 a share? Well, a buyer at that price would be a classic value investor.

● "Contrarian Funds" are difficult to define, but they swim against the tide, buying out-of-favor stocks like value funds and often holding some of their assets in "short positions", which go up when the stock in question goes down— a maneuver that you should never, in our opinion, ever attempt.

● "Socially Responsible Funds," few and far between, invest only in companies that are environmentally and socially responsible.

(3) Details of the stock table:

In our cursory look at the stock table of The Wall Street Journal we ignored several columns with the curious headings "Div", "%", "PE", and "Vol". None of these are essential—or even important—for the beginner, but for the sake of completeness here goes:

52 weeks				Yield		Vol					
Hi	Lo	stock	sym	Div	%	PE	Vol	Hi	Lo	Close	NetChg
29	22 1/2	IBP Inc.	IBP	.10	.4	8	1320	24 1/8	23 7/8	24	-1/8

"**Vol**" refers to the number of shares traded, in hundreds, during a given trading day. On January 14, 1997, 13,200 shares of IBP changed hands.

"**Div**" refers to the dividend paid out by the company yearly to each shareholder. IBP paid out $0.10—not exactly a princely sum—to each shareholder in the past year.

"**%**" simply refers to the percent interest that the dividend on each share represents. Since the price of a share is $24, and $0.10 is paid out to each holder of one share, the percent interest that the shareholder receives is .10/24, or 0.4%

"**PE**" stands for "price-to-earnings ratio," a concept that requires a little explanation. Remember Disco., brainchild and creation of the Nerd family? If in 1997 there are 200,000 Disco. shares, and in 1997 Disco. earns $20,000,000, then the earnings per share are $20,000,000/200,000, or $10. If the stock is selling for $10 per share, then the "price-to-earnings ratio"—i.e., the ratio of the stock price to the earnings per share, is 1. More often PE ratios are 10 to 20, and some "high-flyers," companies whose share prices are highly inflated, can sell for PE ratios of 50, 75, or even much greater.

(4) Bonds: PLEASE *skip this section unless you need a cure for insomnia.*

Bonds make stocks look like a Bruce Willis movie, but nothing will floor parents like these stodgy, gray-haired facts:

When a government or corporation needs to borrow money, it often issues pieces of paper called bonds, which are, in essence, IOU's that pay interest. Large financial organizations sell them to the public (some bonds are sold directly to the public, e.g., U.S. Savings Bonds). In exchange for the use of your money, the corporation or government that issued the bonds pays a fixed dollar amount of interest—printed on the face of the bond—each year, until the bonds "mature," at which time the bonds are redeemed by their current owner, for their "face value," the dollar amount written on the bond.

If AT&T issues a $1000 bond, paying $75 interest each year, maturing in 2005, then anyone owning this bond, from now until 2005, should receive 7.5% interest on his investment per year, right? Not exactly. You see, the bond owner (called the bond "holder") will indeed receive $75 per year, but this sum represents 7.5% of his investment only if he had paid $1000 for the bond. If, for example, the investor had bought the bond for less than its face value, say $900, then the $75 per year would represent 75/900, or 8.33% . But, you may well ask: Why would anyone pay more, or less, than $1000 for a bond that can be redeemed in 2005 for $1000? The answer lies in prevailing interest rates.

Suppose that 2 years after the bond is issued, interest rates in the United States fall, so that bank savings accounts pay only 3%, money market mutual funds 3.7%, and even 2-year bank C.D.'s only 4.2%. Under these circumstances, a bond that pays $75 per year and costs $1000 would be highly desirable, because its interest rate—7.5%—is so much higher than available elsewhere. Naturally, buyers for such bonds appear, and since bonds—like stocks, cars, and jewelry—are worth what people will pay for them, the price of the bond is bid up; people buy the bond for more than its face value, say $1100. (At this price, the interest paid, $75, represents 75/1100, or 6.8%, still much more than the prevailing rate, and the bond price continues to rise, until the interest paid approximates prevailing rates.) **FALLING INTEREST RATES CAUSE A RISE IN BOND PRICES; CONVERSELY, RISING INTEREST RATES REDUCE BOND PRICES.**

This whole scenario is complicated by the fact that at maturity—in our example 2005—the bond will be worth only $1000, because that is all the company initially promised to pay upon maturity. Bond investors and speculators carefully balance these factors in determining what a bond will bring on the open market.

Bond holders can receive interest by mail, or, in the case of "coupon bonds," detach printed coupons actually attached to the bond and redeem these at any bank on specified dates. Coupon bonds are becoming obsolete.

- ●Corporate Bonds are issued by corporations.

- ●Convertible Bonds are complex, because they can be converted at any time to shares of stock of the company that issued them. (We absolutely guarantee that 99.76 % of parents and 99.998% of your friends do not know this fact!). Their value at any given time depends upon both prevailing interest rates and the share price of the "underlying" stock. Ignore convertible bonds.

- ●Municipal Bonds ("Munys") are issued by state and local governments (municipalities). These bonds usually pay a lower interest rate than corporate bonds, but the interest is mostly tax-free—an intentional "loophole" in our tax code, designed to help local governments raise money by issuing bonds, without the financial burden of paying out much interest. Therefore, Munys are best for people in high tax brackets, looking for tax-free interest. Until you are rich, ignore municipal bonds.

●Registered Bonds have the name of the current owner written on them (i.e., they are registered in the owner's name) so they are not easily sold or "fenced" if stolen, but bearer bonds have no such owner designation. Therefore, the bearer—anyone carrying around the bond—can sell it or use it like cash. You guessed it— bearer bonds are the target of choice for big-time thieves and safe crackers! (In the movie Die Hard, the official-looking certificates stolen by the Hans Gruber gang from the vault of the Nakatomi Building were presumably bearer bonds.) PLEASE ignore this fact about bearer bonds!!

If You're Interested:

Louis Rukeyser's Wall Street, 1750 Old Meadow Road, Suite 300, McLean VA, 22102, or LRWS@access.dignex.net., a monthly newsletter, presents a balanced mix of investment advice, both specific (particular stocks, bonds, and mutual funds) and general (trends). Before subscribing to this publication we suggest Wall Street Week with Louis Rukeyser, carried by most PBS channels, Friday evenings. The newsletter is pricy for a beginner; the TV show is free.

Smart Money, The Wall Street Journal's Magazine of Personal Business (1-800-444-4204) published monthly. Lots of investment advice and great information on a variety of other money-saving ideas.

References:

(1) Wall Street Journal Special Supplement, A Century of Investing, Thursday, May 28, 1996, Dow Jones & Company, section R, p. 30.

(2) Wall Street Journal Special Supplement, A Century of Investing, Thursday, May 28, 1996, Dow Jones & Company, section R, p. 45.

(3) Wall Street Journal, Great Stock Pickers? Try Sam Williams, in Fund Track, by Karen Damato, January 23, 1997, Section C, p. 1.

(4) The Wall Street Journal, The Match Game, by Michael Siconolfi and Robert McGough, Tuesday, January 28, 1997, Vol. IC No 19 p 1.

(5) Consumer Reports, How to Choose Mutual Funds, March, 1998.

(6) The Wall Street Journal, Getting Going, by Jonathan Clements, Five Mutual Funds that Can Do It All.

(7) Wall Street Journal Special Supplement, A Century of Investing, Thursday, May 28, 1996, Dow Jones & Company, section R, p. 45.

Chapter 3

Your Individual Retirement Plan:
Retirement Plan? You're Kidding??!!
I'm Just Getting Started??!!

The Minimum Investment Hurdle and the Traditional IRA:

Armed with voluminous information on the practicalities of investing, you now face the most frustrating issue for each beginner: many mutual funds require a minimum investment of $2500; almost all, a minimum of $1000. So, since you don't have $1000 to $2500 (and are unlikely to accumulate this much cash in the near future) are you and the Will Struggleons of the world out of the game? The answer is "**NO!**", but to understand why we have to know a little about retirement plans, Uncle Sam's involvement, and something called a traditional "IRA" (Individual Retirement Plan, pronounced either "I.R.A.", like the Irish Republican Army, or like the name "IRA").

Why the United States Government Got into the IRA Business, and What is a Traditional IRA Anyway?:

For about a generation economists complained that a weakness of the US economy was its low savings rate. "Spendthrift" Americans—relative to the "thrifty" Japanese, for example—put aside too little of their earnings. This low savings rate had all sorts of bad consequences, like a shortage of money (called "capital") to feed economic expansion; so various schemes were suggested to increase the savings rate. Naturally, one incentive would be to permit individuals to establish special accounts with banks, stockbrokers, or mutual fund companies that can hold cash, stocks, bonds, or mutual funds, and to designate the increase in asset value (from rising share prices, dividends, interest, or share trading) **tax free.** At about the same time, concern developed about the long-term viability of Social Security and its ability to support retired individuals. These concerns dovetailed with political agendas that stress individual responsibility and led to the creation of IRA's—individual retirement accounts that accumulate value, year in and year out, "tax deferred"; **"tax deferred" simply means that all tax due is deferred until money is withdrawn from the account. The implications of this creation, as we shall see, are astounding.**

Furthermore, to encourage individuals to establish their own IRA's that will supplement Social Security, contributions of up to $2000 per year are tax deductible for working persons who earn less than $30,000/year, even if they are covered by a company pension plan, and IRA contributions are partially deductible at higher incomes (see CHAPTER 5 for amounts, and the effect of marital status). "Tax deductible" (CHAPTER 5) means that you subtract the amount you put into your IRA from your gross income when you calculate your taxable income; if your taxable income is $20,000/year, without an IRA contribution, and you put $1000 into an IRA, your taxable income falls to $19,000. If you paid 20% of your income in taxes, you would save the 20% that you would have paid on that $1000 contribution—i.e., $200. **Although $2000 is the maximum that you can put into an IRA each year, there is no minimum;** a person working part time, earning $242.87/year delivering newspapers, could legally contribute **the entire $242.87** to an IRA; the amount eligible for contribution equals your gross (pre-tax) earnings, up to the maximum of $2000.

How an IRA Can Overcome the "Minimum Investment" Hurdle:

Although mutual funds almost invariably require a minimum investment of $1000 to $3000 for regular accounts, some will happily establish an IRA for a minimum investment of $500, A FEW FOR EVEN $250!! That means that as soon as you are earning over $250 per year you can join in the mutual fund game. Bank IRA's, in fact, which pay a much lower fixed interest rate (like a savings account) or a slightly variable rate (like a money market mutual fund) will often start you out with as little as $25 to $50!!

Incredibly, The Money Doesn't Really Have to Originate With You!

Now the best part: the contribution to **your** IRA is deductible from **your** taxable income, even if the dollars contributed **did not actually come from your income!!** In other words, if you earn $20,000.00/year and spend every dime in your paycheck, with no cash left to establish an IRA, you are not quite out of luck; **your parents (or anyone else for that matter) can give you up to $2000 to deposit in your IRA; you** make the deposit, then deduct $2000 from your taxable income, saving hundreds of dollars, and you have begun an investment program that will accumulate value, tax deferred, with a big payoff in the future.

But why bother? How big is big?

Gigantic, monstrous, awesome—that's how big!!

Remember, interest, dividends, and increases in asset value of your IRA are tax deferred. If you contribute $500 and the account earns $50/year interest, at the end of the year, the IRA statement will show a value of $550; no tax payments and **no tax reporting** by the individual are required—a tremendous headache relief.

Next year, **even without further contributions**, you will earn interest on the entire $550, and this process, interest compounding, goes on and on. The effect is astounding: **if you contribute $2000 per year to an IRA from age 18 to age 27, and that IRA consistently earns 9% per year, the IRA will be worth close to one million dollars at age 67, even if you never save another nickel past age 27!!** True, your IRA may not earn 9% per year, but then again it might do a lot better, and you expect to keep contributing all along, not stop at 27 (the arbitrary age selected for this interest-compounding example). With any luck at all, a consistent IRA saver will retire with multimillions—a goodly sum, inflation or not.

Is an IRA Right for You Now?

Yes, Yes, and YES!!

You may wonder about an account that cannot be accessed until about age 59, in most circumstances, under current law; we assure you that all of the effects are positive.

(1) You "get into the market"; you follow the value of your IRA account—hopefully an S&P 500 Index fund in the beginning. As the value of the account increases, it will qualify for other mutual funds which have a higher minimum investment. Although there are restrictions on **withdrawals of money from the account, you can easily switch**

from one fund to another fund or to any stockbroker or bank (as long as the account remains an IRA).

(2) The experience you gain from only a few years of IRA-watching will prepare you for investing in regular (not IRA) accounts, with post-tax dollars.

(3) Having an IRA at your age is a badge of responsibility that impresses **everyone**; your significant other's parents, who previously may have considered you a major loser, will drop their jaws at the very mention of an IRA.

(4) **You have a burgeoning retirement system—security for the long future.**

(5) The original purpose of an IRA was to accumulate funds for retirement, so generally speaking withdrawals before age 59 1/2 will incur penalties in addition to taxes, **but the law governing IRA's was revised in 1997, and now the law permits penalty-free withdrawals of up to $10,000 for the purchase of a first home and penalty-free withdrawals with no dollar limit for qualified higher education expenses!** Remember also that a fat IRA account will protect your spouse and family in the event of your death, *so as it builds it can reduce your need for expensive life insurance.*

BUT YOU NEED NOT WAIT UNTIL YOU HAVE FINISHED SCHOOL TO START. Say that you earned $1100 over the summer between your junior and senior year. Your middle names are "Responsibility" and "Self-discipline," so you have saved $507. You can begin an IRA, depositing this money in a wide variety of investment instruments, including an S&P 500 Index Fund. More likely, the $1100 was spent on clothes ($604.78), CD's ($200), dinners out ($200), and the rest on "stuff," but remember that **your parents can give you any** amount up to the total that you earned—in this case $1100—for deposit in your IRA. Assuming that they can afford it, our guess is that your parents will be so floored—stunned, really—that **you are thinking about an IRA**, that **you know what "IRA" means**, that **you have even heard of an IRA**, that they will gratefully contribute to the cause, while thanking The Almighty that their progeny is finally "thinking about the future" and "showing a little responsibility." Try it.

Getting Started:

The largest and best known of the S&P 500 Index Funds, Vanguard, requires a minimum IRA investment of $1000 at the time of this writing, but the Dreyfus S&P 500 Index Fund requires only $750, and the largest "fund family," **Fidelity Investments, includes a no-load fund simply called the "Spartan Market Index Fund," whose minimum investment is only $500.** If you have only $250 to invest, go with the TIAA-CREF Growth and Income fund. (For direct phone numbers, see CHAPTER 2).

Why Not a Bank IRA?

Many banks will open an IRA for a minimum deposit of only $50; you might even find one that will accept $25! But bank IRA's established at these low investment levels are usually committed for a **specific term**—that is, the money must remain in that particular account for a specific agreed-upon length of time, usually one to two years, and the interest paid will lag far, far behind the average returns of an S&P 500 Index Fund. Even if the bank IRA program offers a selection of mutual funds for its IRA's, your chance of outperforming the S&P 500 is low. Therefore: unless your bank allows you access to a no-load S&P 500 Index Fund, we recommend dealing directly with a mutual fund company that offers one, like Dreyfus or Fidelity. But, the supreme advantage of bank IRA's is that money can be deposited directly into the bank IRA from your paycheck, before you ever see it; very few payroll departments, at the present time, make direct deposits into IRA accounts with mutual fund companies, like Fidelity. This is a crucial factor for the poorly motivated saver and may tilt your plan in favor of a bank IRA, at least for the first year or two. **Remember: no matter what anybody tells you, it is *easy* to move money from one IRA to another, so you can *start* with a bank, and when you reach the minimum required for the mutual fund of your choice,** *transfer the money.*

SO:

(1) Any IRA is better than no IRA!

(2) The money doesn't have to originally come from you.

(3) You can start an IRA no matter how low your income.

(4) In most cases the contribution up to $2000 is a tax deduction, and in all cases the interest, dividends, and gains in share value are tax-deferred, compounding for years and years.

(5) Many mutual funds that usually require a hefty initial investment will happily start an IRA account for you with a much lower, affordable contribution.

(6) If at all possible, start with an S&P 500 index fund or start with a bank IRA and switch when your nest egg is large enough. Alternatively, go with the TIAA-CREF Growth and Income Fund.

(7) Relax and smile as your IRA fattens over the years.

A Few Additional Details:

IRA Deductibility:

Even if you are already **covered by a company retirement plan,** IRA contributions *may* be deductible, depending on your "adjusted gross income" (CHAPTER 5). These limits may rise for the next few years, so check with the Internal Revenue Service free information hotline (CHAPTER 5), our recommended books, or tax software, before deciding what limit applies to you.

But keep in mind that **in all cases,** even for the Fat Cat, whose income tops $10,000,000/year, **earnings from an IRA account are tax-deferred.**

Loads, loads, and more loads:

Not all mutual fund sales charges—"loads" as you recall—are alike. Of course, **THE BEST LOAD IS NO LOAD,** and in any account—IRA or non-IRA—money paid up front, called a "front end load," represents a loss to you. Up front loads are often called "A" shares in the mutual fund business. However, many mutual funds also sell "Class B " shares with "deferred sales charges"; in this arrangement all of your initial investment goes to work for you immediately, but a charge is levied if you sell shares within a given time period, usually up to 5 or 6 years (a "rear end load"). After that period has elapsed, the sales charges vanish. For IRA money, which is sure to stay longer than 5 or 6 years, "B" shares would seem to make the most sense, but it turns out that the on-going annual management expenses of "B" shares are greater than for "A" shares! To make matters even more complicated, some funds offer automatic changeover from "B" shares to "A" shares after 5 to 8 years, so you can take advantage of the lower annual "A" share expenses. With all of these complications, our best advice is **stick with no-load funds** unless you have access to a detailed analysis like the annual Smart Money Superstar Funds study, which takes into account all of the various fund expenses and load issues involved.

Other IRA Fees:

Yup, you guessed it, many mutual fund companies and banks charge an annual fee, called a "custodial fee" ($10 to 15 per year), for setting up your IRA, keeping track of the paperwork, and sending you periodic statements. However, you can easily find "no fee IRA's," often at banks. Although a fee of $12/year is quite high, percentagewise, on an account of $250, we do not recommend that the absence of a fee govern your choice of a fund or bank; remember, the custodial fee will, in the worst case, remain fixed at $10-$12 per year, no matter how large the IRA account grows, so after a few years it will become small, then insignificant; in any event, a "no-fee IRA" that grows even a little more slowly than an IRA with a fee is no bargain. Finally, **some aggressive fund companies, like Vanguard, eliminate the custodial fee entirely when your IRA reaches a value of $5000.**

What about the "college IRA" and the "Roth IRA", both creations of the Balanced Budget and Taxpayer Relief Acts of 1997:

(1) **College IRA:** Not for you, unless you have (or soon will have) a child; the "college" in "college IRA" refers to a mechanism that allows you to put aside a small amount of money in a tax-deferred account **for your child's college education.** It won't help **you** with **your own** tuition or college loans.

(2) **Roth IRA:** Named for Senator Roth, this IRA is a radical departure from the "regular IRA" described already. The contribution that you

make to a Roth IRA is **NOT TAX-DEDUCTIBLE**, so unless you are doing very well, you are probably not in a position to establish one; the college student or new graduate usually needs the tax deduction as motivation and financial incentive (see CHAPTER 10, **Putting It All Together**). But, if you can manage to make a **non-deductible contribution**, the interest, dividends, and increased asset value of a Roth IRA is **tax FREE**—not "tax-deferred"—**for ever and ever!!!** In other words, you pay no tax—even upon withdrawal. Head-to-head comparisons between "regular" and "Roth" IRA's, at age 59 1/2, when withdrawals begin, show a substantial advantage to the Roth plan. So go with Roth if you can afford to miss the initial tax deduction.

Conclusion: When you are starting out, use the traditional IRA if you have to (most people do), but use the Roth system if you can afford it— i.e., when you don't need the tax deduction. Even if you can't afford the Roth system now, start one in addition to your regular IRA in a few years, when you can.

Appendix: So How do the Dow Diamonds and "spiders" fit into the picture?

The strength of these two investment options is that you can buy as little as one share of either; the weakness is that they are bought through stockbrokers, and most stockbrokers require that your account have a minimum starting balance of $2000. However, the competition among discount brokers is keen, and trading fees (what you pay in commissions to the broker above and beyond the price of a stock) have recently plummeted; many observers predict that within 2 to 3 years the minimum starting balance in most brokerage accounts will also fall, perhaps as low as $500. Currently, National Discount Brokers (NDB.com) will open an account for you with no minimum initial investment and no minimum monthly balance. Therefore, the DOW Diamonds and "spiders" represent a practical alternative to an S&P 500 Index Fund, **and the more you invest the better this alternative becomes.** Why? Because the sales charge (commission) for a stock purchase of $250, at National Discount Brokers, is $14.95, or 5.98%, **and the sales charge remains the same for larger purchases.** In other words, the commission for purchase of stock worth $1000 remains $14.95—now only 1.49%. At this rate, the purchase of "spiders" approaches the yearly management/overhead cost of a no load S&P 500 Index Fund, and the choice between these two options depends upon the annual IRA fee charged by the Fund versus that of the Broker. Check it out. *You win big, either way.*

Facts That Will Impress Your Parents:

This whole chapter—any sentence in it—will do the trick!

Chapter 4

Checking Accounts: For You or Against You

Six-thirty p.m. and Will Struggleon is heading home, after a ten-hour day filing delinquent account reports at Paypoor Inc. Empty of wallet and stomach, too tired to cook and sick of frozen dinners, Will visits the corner ATM before picking up a Coke, burger, and fries, and being a frugal soul, knowing that money withdrawn is usually money spent, carefully withdraws only $10. Will plans to eat for $3, buy $5 worth of gas, and rent a video for $2, only slightly denting the $50 that remains in the checking account, which has to last 4 more days until payday.

So far, so good? No, not really, **not good at all**. Because, sad to say, Will paid the equivalent of $11.75 for $10 worth of food and gas! **The ATM was not owned by Will's bank but was part of the world-wide ATM "network"; for using a network ATM, Will's account was hit with a $.75 fee by his own bank and another $1 charge from the bank that owns the ATM! These fees are euphemistically called "surcharges."**

Will has been desperately trying to "get ahead"—to have a little left over each month, for saving, investing, or luxuries, and so has developed the apparently admirable habit of withdrawing **small** amounts from an ATM **every few days,** never denting the balance significantly or risking excessive cash expenditures, **but the result has been disaster.** Three

ATM visits per week (two withdrawals and one deposit) add up to $5.25 in fees, creating a monthly hemorrhage of $21, enough to pay the phone bill, 4 days of groceries, or a dinner out. Seen another way, on this exhausting day Will put in 2 hours of overtime at "time and one-half"; at the hourly salary of $5.20, the ATM charge and surcharge ate 13.5 minutes of that 2-hour overtime stint. Will is working, at least part of the time, for the bank.

THE PROBLEM: In the Dark Ages before ATM's, people got money for the week by cashing a check at the bank or withdrawing money from a savings account. These transactions were inconvenient but inexpensive (no fee for a savings account withdrawal or cashed paycheck, $0 to $.50 for cashing a personal check, depending upon the type of account). Because of the inconvenience, trips to the bank were once- on the corner! Even fast food restaurants are now extending this trend, with in-store ATM's.

The ATM habit has been fostered by banks, which often permit free ATM transactions on student checking accounts, so that after a few years of college you are "hooked," only to find that after college few checking accounts are so benign. Remember: after student days the ATM is a budget buster, *unless you use your bank's own machine and have the right kind of checking account.* Try to think of ATM's as card-operated bandits that pick your pocket of $1 to$2 each time you withdraw. And, with each passing year, ATM fees are rising…

O.K., O.K., I get the picture, checking accounts that charge ATM fees are a bummer…what do I do?

Traditional finance books begin by listing the many fees associated with most checking accounts and then advising you to shop around and find an account that minimizes or eliminates them. Superficially rational, the problem with this approach is that you could end up with a dream account—no fees for each check you write, no fees for transactions at the bank's own ATM, no minimum balance, no monthly maintenance fee—and still get killed if the ATM you use is not owned by your bank! *So, we suggest that you start at the other end, scoping out the location of ATM's that you will really use, and then checking to see if a bank that owns any one of these machines offers a checking account with free transactions at its own ATM's.*

Great! My neighborhood has 5 ATM's. What do I check out at each bank?

Checking accounts are crammed with hidden fees, usually in very small print on colorful glossy brochures. A **partial** fee list includes: a charge for using the bank's own ATM, a surcharge for using another bank's ATM or a "network" ATM, a fee for writing each check or a fee for writing more than a limited number of checks permitted by that particular type of account, a fee for letting your balance (the amount of money you have in the account at any time) fall below a minimum, a monthly "maintenance fee," as well as fees for bounced checks, "stop payment" orders, and even a fee for depositing someone else's bad check—as if you knew it was bad! (Incidentally, a "stop payment" order means that you write a check and then decide to make it invalid, so you call the bank and tell it to stop payment; this "stiffs" the person you wrote the check to, so you'd better have a good reason and wear bullet-proof underwear. A "bounced check" is a check that was written when the account didn't have enough money to "cover" the check—for example, you write a check for $100 and your account balance is only $90—**BAD IDEA!**)

But, don't despair. Mercifully, not all fees are equal, not all checking accounts are equal, and not all banks are equal. **You need to start by reducing or eliminating the fees that relate to you: fees for ATM use**

and for writing each check. (After all, you could easily interact with an ATM two to three times a week for a year and write 15 checks a month but never stop payment on a check).

As you probably know but have taken for granted so far, **many banks offer "dream" checking accounts to students;** one bank features a student checking account that requires a minimum average balance of $200 (if the balance falls below that level, a monthly fee of $2 is charged), unlimited withdrawals and deposits at the bank's own ATM'S, and an unlimited number of checks, with no fee per check. The minimum balance requirement is waived for July, August, and September. Not all student accounts are at "megabanks"; for example, a smaller bank (New York City Area) features a "Student Privilege Account" with no minimum balance, eight free checks per month, and UNLIMITED TRANSACTIONS AT THE BANK'S OWN ATM'S. **(Note: rumor has it that nobody at most banks checks to see if you have graduated, so you should start this type of account while you are still at school, if you possibly can, and drag it out until you are asked for verification of continued student status, hopefully years down the line. This maneuver is legal.)**

In addition, a few highly-competitive consumer-oriented banks offer "dream accounts" to *non-students:* for example, at least one bank offers the "Positively Free Checking Account"—no minimum balance, no per check fee (up to 25 checks per month), and unlimited free transactions at the bank's own ATM'S.

With a student account or similar "dream account" you can withdraw small amounts at a time from your bank's ATM and avoid the temptation to spend "extra" cash in your pocket, but *try, try, and try to avoid transactions at other bank's or network machines, which will incur surcharges in virtually any account.*

Cool!! But what do I do if the five or six convenient ATM's near my job or house belong to banks with checking accounts that charge me a fee each time I feed in my plastic card?

This is the financial equivalent of a leap from the Empire State Building—nowhere to go but down. Rescue options include:

(1) Fast forward to the past and kick the ATM habit! Deposit your paycheck in person (no charge), but make the deposit slip out for less than the full amount of your check and receive the difference in cash (usually no charge). Or sign up for a **savings account** with "direct deposit"—your employer sends the check electronically to the account (no charge)—and you withdraw cash personally (no charge) at the bank. This routine is easier said than done, because bank hours usually coincide with work hours (who wants to stand in line during lunch break?), ATM's may be close to work but a bank itself may be too far, and having a week's worth of cash without running through it is like serving pizza "with everything" at a Weight Watcher's convention and expecting attendees to each eat 1/128 of a slice. This system has a much better chance of working if you can find a bank in your neighborhood that is open late one evening and on Saturday morning; then, you can make several personal transactions each week, without fees, and resist squandering only 3-4 day's worth of cash at a time. But in all honesty, the likelihood that you will do **any** personal banking, with its long lines and inconveniences, is almost nil.

(2) If each ATM in your work or home neighborhood charges a fee, and if you run through more than two day's worth of cash like water through a sieve, then find a checking account that lets you write the largest number of free checks per month, so you can minimize ATM transactions by paying almost everything by check. Simplify your life by signing up for "direct deposit" of your paycheck into the checking account. Even if you exceed the maximum number of free checks per-

mitted by your account, the fee per additional check (usually $0.25 to $0.35 per check) is far less than the $1 to $2 levied for network ATM's. Unfortunately, many sellers—like gas stations—hesitate to take a personal check.

(3) Use a debit card. You can also minimize dependence on ATM visits with a "debit card" and/or a credit card, but each of these can create more problems than they solve. (We cover credit cards in chapter seven, but be forewarned—the risks involved with debit cards are far, far greater than risks with credit cards, so, convenient as they are, **every debit card owner must be security conscious** *in the extreme.*)

So what is a debit card?

A "*debit card*" is a plastic card that looks like a credit or ATM card but when used for purchases the item's price *is electronically subtracted from your checking account at the bank,* so, after using the card, you must subtract the cost of the purchase from the balance in your checkbook "register" (explained on the next page), or you will soon carelessly bring your checking account balance to zero! Most checking accounts come with debit cards and permit unlimited debit card transactions for a single low fee (usually about $1 per month). So, you could visit an ATM once per week, withdraw only a modest amount of cash, and pay for almost everything else with the debit card, saving your free checks for bills like rent, phone, and electricity. Sounds good, but trouble from a debit card can be only a few mishaps away.

Staying out of trouble with a checking account and debit card— the check "register":

When you start a checking account, you receive a supply of blank checks and a blank "check register," which has columns already labeled (if the columns are not already labeled, write in these labels yourself, at the top):

To begin using the account, we'll start by depositing $104 in cash at the bank on 1/1/00 and then paying your first bill, $18.70, for electricity, on the same day.

Check "Number"	Date	Transaction Description	Payment	Deposit	Balance
	1/1/00	*Deposit Cash*		104.00	104.00
1	1/1/00	*Electric Bill*	18.70		-18.70
					85.30

"Check Number " is the number on the check; in this example, we are writing our first check, #1.

"Date" is the date you make a deposit or write a check.

"Transaction Description" is essential for your records and sanity; this is what the check is for; in this case, the electric bill.

"Balance" is the amount of money that remains in the account.

TO STAY OUT OF TROUBLE:

(1) Always subtract the amount of the check from the last balance , so your new balance is actually what you have left in the account. Here we subtract $18.70 from $104.00, ending with a balance of $85.30.

(2) Always keep your ATM withdrawal or deposit receipts, and enter the transaction into the register as soon as possible.

(3) Do the same with debit card payments, because these are electronically subtracted from your balance when you use the card.

The check itself is self-explanatory, but be sure to enter what the check is for in the lower left hand corner, in a space usually called "memo" or "for".

I.will Struggleon
000 Future Rd.
Workville, NY   **1/ 1/ 00**
00000

Pay to the
order of: *The Electric Company*_____   **$ 18.70**

_____ *Eghteen Dollars and seventy cents*_____

For___ *Electricity*_____   *I. Will Struggleon*

At the end of the month, your bank will send you a packet that includes all of the checks you have written that have been cashed (or paid by your bank). Believe it or not, once a check has been cashed, it is called a **"canceled check"**; this does **not** mean that anything is wrong with the check or that payment has been stopped—it is simply the jargon of banking. You can use a "canceled check" as proof that you paid for something, because it indicates that the recipient deposited it and it was paid by your bank. Thus, when you order items by mail you often see the notation "your canceled check is your receipt"—in other words, you will receive no receipt from the seller as proof of payment, but your canceled check will do.

In the packet with your canceled checks is the bank "statement" that lists all checks presented to your bank for payment and all fees charged to your account. Here is where you will feel the bite of multiple ATM transactions, too many checks, a balance below the minimum, etc. At this point you "balance" the account: see the appendix for the least tedious balancing method.

A cash deposit is straightforward, but, in fact, few people ever deposit cash, and to deposit a check you need a little information, rarely provided by your friendly bank:

(1) Endorsing a check: To prevent anyone who finds a check made out to you from depositing it, you must sign the back of the check (called "endorsing the check") with your name, exactly as it appears on the check. *Failure to endorse the check may prevent it from going through the bank (clearing) and being credited to your account.* When you endorse, be precise; if a check is made out to " I.Will Struggleon", a signature on the back that says "W. Struggleon" may be considered invalid. To endorse, you must sign the check on the back, **across the top of the short end, often above a line that says "endorse above this line".**

For example:

```
 _I. Will Struggleon_
 Endorse above this line
```

"**Endorsing over a check**": If a check is made out to you, say by your room mate, for $100, and you owe $100 to somebody else (Joe Doakes, for example), you can assign the check to Joe, by "endorsing it over" to him. Simply write "pay to Joe Doakes" across the top of the short end, on the back, and sign below that statement:

```
Pay to Joe Doakes
  I. Will Struggleon
Endorse above this line
```

(3) **Check "clearing"**: You deposit a salary check of $450 on Friday, bringing your low balance of $50 up to $500. The next day, Saturday, you sit down and pay the pile of bills that has been threatening to collapse the kitchen table. Your write 5 checks, totaling $450, and mail them. They are delivered on Monday, and **most of them bounce. Why? Because when you deposit a check in the bank you must usually wait 3 to 5 "business days" (Monday through Friday) for your check to "clear," i.e., to be credited to your checking account.**

(4) **"Bouncing" a check**: Hopefully, you will never "bounce" a check, the polite term for writing a check that cannot be cashed by the recipient, because your checking account has insufficient funds to pay it—i.e., to "cover" it. In such a case you will be charged a "bad check" fee, and even if somebody else's check bounces when **you** try to deposit it in **your** account, you will be charged a fee!! And, the merchant to whom you wrote the bounced check can assess a fat fee for his/her inconvenience—$10 to $25!

The usual reason for a "bounced check" is insufficient funds, but other reasons include "uncollected funds", illegible signature, contradiction between written amount and numerical amount, account closed, payment stopped, missing endorsement, endorsement does not match name of payee, dated in the future, check "stale"—i.e., over 30-90 days old (depending on your bank), etc. Of these reasons, two require amplification:

(a) **Uncollected funds:** If you have already deposited enough money to "cover" a check, but a check you write on these funds is presented to the bank before the check you deposited has cleared, you have funds on record in your account, but they have not actually been collected by your bank. The funds are not exactly "insufficient" but are "uncollected". This fine distinction matters not at all when the check bounces, but at least it reassures you that you **have** made the right deposits and simply need to wait a few days for the deposited checks to "clear"—i.e., to be credited.

(b) **Stopped payment:** Suppose you pay for an item by check and then decide that you have been ripped off. Negotiations are futile. You can call your bank and ask that payment be stopped on the check you wrote; there will be a modest fee for this service, but it will work almost all of the time, especially if you provide your bank with the check number, date, amount, and payee. Then, when the crook who ripped you off attempts to deposit or cash the check, it will bounce! But be careful; unless you are clearly in the right, legal action against you may force you to pay. Stopping payment is a good financial weapon to know about and rarely use.

Note that some checking accounts let you write checks for more than your balance, called an "overdraft privilege"; in these cases, the bank will honor checks that would "bounce" if written on an ordinary account, but the money provided by the bank to cover your indiscretion is **basically an automatic loan,** with fees and/or a **high interest rate.** We do not recommend these accounts; they are an invitation to major problems.

Paying bills by mail, using standard paper checks:

Almost any bill has two parts, a top part (the "stub") that you return with your check, and a bottom part that you keep for your records. On the stub you fill in the amount you are paying—hopefully the entire amount owed, and often the stub must be positioned in the return envelope so as to show the company's address through a transparent envelope "window." The stub assists a business in logging in your payment, so be sure to include it. As we will see below, one of the disadvantages of "digital" or "on-line checking" is the absent stub, which can slow the payment process considerably and incur late charges.

"On Line" or "PC" Banking: A better way?

The likelihood that you enjoy fooling with piles of paper, wasting valuable time mailing letters, and constantly running out of stamps is low, and the likelihood that you are "on line" (or will soon be "on line") is very high. So, why not use your personal computer to pay bills electronically and avoid a significant hassle?

"On line banking," also called "digital checking," works with either stand-alone free software provided by your bank or one of the popular personal finance programs like Microsoft Money or Quicken, along with a subscription to an electronic bill-paying service, like Check-Free (1).

Software from your own bank gives you instant access to your checking account, so as you authorize a payment the sum will be immediately subtracted from your account (i.e., your account will be "debited"), and the remaining money (the balance) will automatically be updated; this way you know what you have at all times.

Quicken or Microsoft Money can integrate investment accounts, savings, and checking into one grand plan, but because a third-party bill-paying service sits between you and the payment, your account is not debited until you receive a printed statement at the end of the month (1).

Cool! Good-bye paper checks!

Not so fast! To date, some major billers (charge card companies, department stores, etc.) were set up to accept payment directly, electronically, from on-line digital payers. So how do the others get paid? Believe it or not, your bank or on-line bill-paying service will receive your electronic message *and then send a paper check, through the mail, to pay the bill!* Why would the bank take on the hassle that you are trying to avoid? Because the cost to the bank of processing a direct electronic payment is a tiny fraction of the cost of processing a paper check that you write and send; therefore, the banks are trying, with all of their considerable influence, to spread digital checking throughout the galaxy, at warp speed, to hasten the day when everybody—merchants, doctors, massage parlors—will accept direct digital payments.

Unfortunately, the "stub" that you would include with your paper check does not accompany a paper check sent by the bank (since you authorized payment digitally, without mailing the "stub" that is attached to each bill). This omission may delay crediting your payment, so, to avoid a "late charge," **you will have to pay the bill digitally at least five days before it is due**; last minute digital payments are an invitation to trouble. (Most banks will reimburse you for such late charges, but few will help if you goof and send funds to the wrong address, where they become lost in cyberspace, difficult to find, nearly impossible to retrieve). Even worse, many bill paying services and/or banks charge a monthly fee from $5 to $20 per month!

Therefore:

(1) Go to on-line digital checking only if bank software is free, and the bank charges no monthly fee. Be sure that there is no fee for each electronic payment made.

(2) For the beginner, working with Quicken, Money, etc. in conjunction with a pricey bill-paying service is usually an unnecessary complication and expense.

(3) Start slowly, paying only one or two bills per month, until you are familiar with the system.

(4) Pay bills five days before they are due to avoid late charges and the hassle of recovering these charges from the bank.

What about interest?

In our view, focusing on the interest paid by a checking account is like worrying about the dance band on the Titanic. Your goal in selecting a checking account is to avoid substantial chronic fees; the amount of interest that you would gain in one account versus another is far, far less important than free ATM transactions, a low required minimum balance, low or absent maintenance fees, and a generous allotment of free checking or debit card transactions.

Credit Cards: Yup, it's true, much as we hate to admit it, credit cards are an indispensable part of everybody's finances. Without one it's actually impossible to rent a car in most states, and staying in a hotel can be difficult if you can't show plastic. (Don't even think of trying to pay with a check!) But, you already have plenty to worry about, without credit card debt, so we advise a breathing space of six to twelve months before you succumb. In CHAPTER 7 we'll go over the topic, keeping you out of trouble, and avoiding major rip-offs.

The Bottom Line: Kick the ATM habit or work around it, with smart debit card use. Use free "on line" banking if possible, to cut hassle. **Don't** let a checking account work against you when it can work for you.

SECURITY PRECAUTIONS FOR DEBIT AND ATM CARDS

Usually, an ATM card and a debit card are physically one and the same; when you interact with an ATM, the card becomes an "ATM" card, and when you pay for something it becomes a debit card; you "swipe" the card through a card reader, select the "debit option," *and supposedly enter your personal identification number (PIN)*. In fact, very few stores require the pin when a debit card is used to buy something. This alarming fact enables a thief who steals your debit card to go on a spending binge, limited only by the amount of money in your checking account (plus your line-of-credit)!

Do you have any real protection against financial loss if your debit card (or card and PIN) are stolen? Well, the burden is on you—to inform the card issuer (usually a bank) IMMEDIATELY! Most banks will limit your loss to $50, *if they are called within two business days of your learning of the loss or theft,* but your loss could be as much as $500 if you do not call the card issuer within two business days after learning of the loss or theft. And, if you see on your bank statement an unauthorized transfer of funds out of your account, call immediately; if you call over 60 days after the statement is mailed to you, you can face UNLIMITED LOSS—everything in your account and the overdraft as well. So review your bank statement within a day or two of its arrival, and let the bank know if anything is awry.

Therefore:

(1) Report lost or stolen credit or ATM/debit cards or your PIN immediately. Most banks and credit card companies have extended telephone customer service hours; the bank's phone number is on the monthly bank statement. Don't put it off until tomorrow. When you call, the bank will electronically cancel the ATM/Credit card, and your checking account will be safe. Another card will be issued promptly.

(2) Guard your PIN. Memorize your PIN. DO NOT keep a copy of your PIN in your wallet or purse. Tell NO ONE your PIN.

(3) When your ATM card is issued, you will be asked to sign a form that extends its use to debit card; decline if you are forgetful and lose things often. Having an ATM card does NOT require you to select the debit option.

(4) SAVE ALL ATM RECEIPTS; they are excellent records of, and proof of, transactions. Remember, these little slips of paper tell what you've deposited or withdrawn and often tell your balance too. Anybody who picks one up knows much more about your financial life than he should, making you an easy target for scams and schemes, not to mention violence.

Appendix: BALANCING YOUR CHECKING ACCOUNT:

> We recommend that you skip this appendix during your first read and continue on to get the big picture, but sooner or later (hopefully sooner) return to this section for the least tedious balancing routine.

Why?

Balancing a checking account combines the anxiety of skating on thin ice with the boredom of reading a telephone book. So, you may well ask, *since nobody makes you balance your account, why voluntarily play the game?* We answer: *because money is no game.* Banks make mistakes, people make mistakes, even calculators and computers can make mistakes, and mistakes with your money can cost you time, energy, and dollars. The entire exercise is designed to catch errors—the bank's, yours, anybody's—before they catch you.

When your checking account is about a month old you receive an envelope from the bank with a "bank statement" and explicit instructions on the reverse side that walk you through "the balancing act." Stop! Do not proceed upon pain of death by boredom! The "explicit instructions" assume that you already know some crucial definitions, and they never deal with why you are doing what you are doing, a sure-fire way to leave you confused and unmotivated.

So what's it all about?

Whenever you write a check you subtract the amount of that check from the balance in your checkbook register, and the balance falls; when you make a deposit, the balance rises. So far, so good. But other transactions at the bank, "behind the scenes." affect your real balance, and you do not see these transactions until you see your statement. For example, payment of interest into your checking account—an unlikely scenario for low-balance accounts—increases the balance, whereas ATM fees, monthly "maintenance fees" and individual check-writing fees reduce it. **Therefore, your check register balance may not correspond to what you really have in the bank!**

Also, some checks you wrote had probably not been paid by your bank at the time your statement was printed; if not, these checks reduce the balance on your register, but not in your bank's computer. In financial jargon, such checks have not been "posted" and are called "outstanding," a word that does not refer to quality, like "excellent," or "awesome," or "superior"—but means checks that are "standing out there," waiting to be presented to your bank for payment.

Confused? You write a $350 check to Mom for rent on your apartment in her basement (just a temporary arrangement, of course) and a $50 check to cousin Vinnie (so he can rent a limo and impress his lady friend). Mom, true to form, takes your check to the bank before the ink is dry, but Vinnie and his girl break up, so he leaves the check in his dresser drawer and forgets to tell you (also true to form). The check promptly cashed by Mom has been posted and will lower the balance in both your bank and your own register by $350.00, but Vinnie's check is still "outstanding," so it lowers the balance on your register but not (yet) in the bank.

The mission of the "balancing act" is to seek out all transactions for the previous month, correct all errors, and boldly go where few students or new graduates have gone before—to financial reality. You reach this coveted state by adjusting your register balance, factoring in additions and subtractions from "behind the scenes," and also adjusting the bank's version of your balance by subtracting checks outstanding. Then, your revised register balance and the adjusted bank balance will match.

Incidentally, a check is posted at the bank when it is logged into the bank's computer. But, if there is something wrong with the check (illegible, discrepant numerical and written-out amounts, insufficient funds to "cover" the check, etc.) it will be posted but not paid. Such "bad checks" will be immediately mailed separately to you and will be flagged on the bank statement. So, if you haven't written or deposited any bad checks or received any back in the mail, you can safely assume that a posted check has been paid by your bank.

The bank statement—take a deep breath, grit your teeth, and look:

A bank statement is an intimidating document, characterized by confusing layout, small print, and undefined terms, but it is a mine of information. All statements list your name and address, account number, beginning balance, inclusive dates covered, deposits and other additions (like interest paid), withdrawals and other subtractions (various fees and checks posted), and the final balance (Figure 1). Remember: unless you are informed otherwise, **a check posted has been paid by your bank.**

The Great American Balancing Act:

Step (1): Circle *each item* that appears in *both* your check register and under "transactions" on the statement. Mark each *uncircled item* on your register and statement with a star, preferably in color, as a "flag." The circled items require no further attention. Also flag any discrepant amounts for the same transaction, for example, if your register says you paid Joe's garage $210 and the bank deducted $220; take a look at your canceled check, enclosed with the statement, for the correct figure, and fix your register or call the bank as indicated. Also look closely at ATM transactions, and flag discrepancies; often you will have logged in your checkbook register an ATM withdrawal of $20 for example, only to find a deduction of $21 on your statement! The extra dollar is an ATM fee that you need to subtract from your register, along with other fees, later. (Incredibly, ATM fees are usually **not** listed separately on your statement, so a $1 fee on a $20 withdrawal simply appears as a subtraction of $21. By "flagging" such items you will immediately see the ATM fees you will have to deal with.) CONFUSED?? Hold on…This will start to make sense as we slog through Figures 1 and 2.

On the enclosed sample register (figure 2) we have flagged check # 3, ($42, for Cable TV), check #6 ($50 for Cousin Vinnie), an ATM transaction on 1/15/00 for $20, and a deposit of $1000 on 1/31/00. The two checks and the deposit of $1000 are "flagged" on the register, because they do not appear on the statement, and the ATM withdrawal of $20 on 1/15/00 is flagged because it is discrepant—the statement lists an ATM withdrawal on that date of $21 (Figure 1).

On the Bank statement (Figure 1) we have flagged the discrepant ATM withdrawal of $21 on 1/15/00 and two fees—a $15 maintenance fee (balance fell too low) and a check writing fee of $0.75 (one check over the freebie limit of four)—Figure 1.

Already you have some practical, perhaps profitable information: Cousin Vinnie's check has not been posted and is outstanding. Maybe Vinnie lost it, or decided that he didn't need it, or is holding it to cash later, for purposes not originally intended. Give Vinnie a call, and you might get back $50. In a more serious scenario, important checks that you made out to stores, or utilities, or a charge card company may be outstanding; usually, companies take two to four days to deposit or cash your check, so if you paid bills within three or four days of the last day covered by your statement, the recipients may not have had time to cash them and you shouldn't worry, but if you have any checks outstanding that were written 10 days or more before the last day covered by your statement, there may be a problem: Was the check lost? Did you actually forget to mail it?

Better look into the outstanding check to Time-Warner Cable. Call Customer Service at your bank (open long after usual business hours) and tell them your problem, as specifically as possible, for example: I have account number _____, social security number _____, and my name is _____. My last bank statement covers 1/1/00 to 1/31/00. I wrote a check for $42 to Time-Warner for cable TV on 1/10/00, check number 3. This check does not appear on my statement as posted, so it was still outstanding at the time of my statement. Does your computer show that it has posted after my statement was printed? If the response is "yes, the check has been posted", all is well, but if the response is "I'm sorry, check number 3 has not been posted to date", you should call again every few days for a week, and then, if the check remains outstanding, assume something is wrong. Call the party to whom you wrote the check. You may have to write another check and ask the bank to "stop payment" on check # 3, a maneuver that costs $10 to $15.

What else can you learn from the simple flag on transactions that do not appear in both your register and the bank statement? You get to see, up close, all "behind the scenes" costs to your account— ATM fees, check writing fees, maintenance fees, etc. Maybe it's time to change banks, or at least ATM's.

Step (2): Use the asterisk "flags" to identify transactions you will now work with. Put a line through each item after you deal with it (not done on our sample, for purposes of legibility).

Step(3): Adjust your checkbook register (see worksheet): In your check register, update the balance, by first **ADDING** any deposits shown on the statement but not in your register (you may have forgotten to add them to your checkbook register at the time of deposit) and any interest that was paid to your account (assuming you have an interest-earning account). Then **SUBTRACT** any checks that you forgot to subtract from your register when you wrote the check (yes, that does happen, even to the best of us), any service charges or fees laid on by the bank, and any automatic deductions (like an automatic investment plan or automatic loan payment). In our example we subtract three fees, an ATM fee of $1 (which explains the discrepant ATM withdrawals on 1/15/00), a check writing fee of $0.75, and a maintenance fee of $15, for a total of $16.75, from the balance of $1100; the resulting balance is **$1083.25.** Hang on. *You are approaching financial reality at Warp speed.*

Step (4): Update your bank balance:

List all "outstanding checks" (flagged in your checkbook register and absent from the statement) and add these up; on our register we have two "outstanding checks," $50 to cousin Vinnie and $42 to Time Warner Cable, for a total of $92. Subtract the total of these two checks from the final bank balance on your statement; in our example the balance of $175.25 falls to $83.25. (We are subtracting these outstanding checks, because they will soon be posted and paid, lowering your true bank balance). Then **add** all deposits shown in your register but not on the statement; here we add a deposit of $1000, so the total rises to **$1083.25.**

(In our case the deposit was made after the statement was printed, and in all probability this is the explanation for a "missing" deposit when the deposit date is close to or after the last date of the statement, but the bank **could** have failed to credit a deposit that you made!! If you think this has happened, call Customer Service at once and ask for your current balance and a record of the month's deposits. If the bank really failed to record a deposit (an extremely rare event), use your ATM transaction receipt as proof of the disputed deposit (this is one reason why you save all ATM receipts). **Insist upon a revised written statement before proceeding.**

Step (5): The balancing act is complete—record your victory:

The updated checkbook register balance should now exactly match the modified bank balance (in our example, it does) because you have updated your check register balance for "behind the scenes" subtractions and additions, and adjusted your bank balance by subtracting outstanding checks. In the jargon of finance the account is "reconciled!" This figure is the true amount you have to work with, because it accounts for all additions, subtractions, and checks outstanding.

Write "balanced" in your register across from the updated amount. Along the way you have become aware of checks that were written but not cashed, fees that sneak by us all, any deposits or withdrawals you might have neglected to enter in your register, and any bank errors in crediting your deposits. Congratulations!!

OOPS! Out of balance:

(1) Check your math, all of it, with a calculator, twice.

(2) Call the bank. Ask about any transactions you don't understand.

(3) Repeat the process, **thinking about what you are doing as you do it.**

If you're interested:

Consumer Reports, August, 1997, pp. 54-55.

Figure 1

Bank Statement

Type of Account:	Account Number:	Dates:
Basic	000-00-000	01/01/00-01/31/00

Name: I .Will Struggleon

**Address: 000 Future Rd.
Workville, NY.   00000**

Date Posted	Description of Transactions	Checks andOther Subtractions	Deposits and Other Additions	Balance
01/01/00	Deposit		1000.00	1000.00
01/04/00	Check #1	350.00		650.00
01/10/00	Cash Withdrawal, Times Square ATM	100.00		550.00
01/13/00	Check #2	45.00		505.00
01/15/00	Cash ATM Withdrawal, Queens Blvd *	21.00		484.00
01/16/00	Check # 4	24.00		460.00
01/21/00	Check # 5	39.00		421.00
01/02/00	Cash Withdrawal Times Square ATM	20.00		401.00
01/27/00	Check # 7	210.00		191.00
01/27/00	Maintenance fee: Balance below 300.00 on 1/27/00 *	15.00		176.00
01/31/00	Check writing fee: one check over max of 4/month*	.75		175.25

Figure 2
Checkbook Register

Check Number	Date	Trasaction Description	Payments		Deposits	Balance
	1/1/00	Deposit $1000.00			$1000.00	$1000.00
1	1/4/00	Rent, Mom	350	00		-350.00 650.00
2	1/8/00	Electric Company	45	00		-45.00 605.00
3	1/10/00	Time-Warner Cab.TV *	42	00		-42.00 563.00
	1/10/00	ATM	100	00		-100.00 463.00
4	1/12/00	Phone Company (local)	24	00		-24.00 439.00
	1/15/00	ATM, not my Bank*	20	00		-20.00 419.00
5	1/13/00	Sprint, long distance	39	00		-39.00 380.00
6	1/18/00	Cousin Vinnie*	50	00		-50.00 330.00
	1/22/00	ATM	20	00		-20.00 310.00
7	1/26/00	Joe's Garage	210	00		-210.00 100.00
	1/31/00	Deposit $1000*			$1000.00	+1000.00 1100.00

Chapter 5

The Basics of Taxes:
Boring Stuff that Shouldn't Keep You Up at Night

You've heard the old line "nothing is certain but death and taxes." Well, with cryogenics and cloning, death may not be so certain. But taxes...at least for your working career will be with us. So, you should understand how taxes affect you, and what you can (legally) do about them. (However, as we said at the very end of CHAPTER 1, although the principles of the tax code remain constant, the details are in a state of constant evolution, so you'll need to look at the updated material we recommend to get the details straight for the current tax year.)

I work for my money—I don't rely on the government. So why should I have to pay taxes?

First, simply because the law (Sixteenth Amendment to the U.S. Constitution) says so. Beware of any schemes that call federal taxes unconstitutional and claim that you need not file. Such challenges have been consistently rejected by the courts; failure to pay may result in stiff penalties and fines (and in some cases, prison).

But, in fact, the truth is that we all use government services. Yes, your federal taxes go for defense, but they also go for air traffic controllers, food inspectors, medical research, national parks, and other items that directly or indirectly benefit you. State taxes go for roads, licensing of doctors, state universities, etc. City and local taxes maintain libraries, police and fire departments, schools, garbage collection, and many other essentials.

So, yes, most of us have to pay taxes. This chapter will help you comply with the law while reducing the amount you pay to the legal minimum.

I'm going to hire a pro, or use tax software on my new laptop, so why do I have to slog through this chapter?

Professional tax preparers vary enormously, and the most careful and knowledgeable can best minimize your tax bill *when you provide lots of documentation and ask the right questions.* To take full advantage of the professional you are paying for, you need to know the basics.

Tax software (discussed later) is pretty good, but familiarity with basic tax jargon is essential before you start. In any case, you can rationally plan to reduce next year's tax bill only if you know how the system works.

Okay, I'm stuck, but where do I go to check out the innumerable regulations and exceptions that may apply to me?

For free help we recommend the IRS website and IRS office or toll-free number (pinpointed later); otherwise, any standard Income Tax guide is a good source.

When and what do I do?

The "when" is easy—you "file" every year by April 15 (sometimes a few days later, if April 15 isn't a workday, but it's easier to just remember April 15). "File" means complete a form and send it (manually, electronically or telephonically, as we will see later) to the Government. The part of the federal Government that processes federal tax returns is called the Internal Revenue Service and is an agency of the Treasury Department.

Suppose you absolutely *can't* make the deadline. In school, you could get an incomplete. You can also do that with the Government, provided you file a form 4868, requesting an automatic extension. But if you owe money, you will have to pay interest (and possibly a penalty on top of that) for any delays after the actual filing due date.

"What" do you do to file? Part of the job is already done by your employer and anywhere you invest (bank, mutual fund, etc.) During the year, as we saw in Chapter 1, your employer deducts taxes from your salary and deposits these with the Government. At year end (actually in January of the new year), your employer will send you a form called a "W-2" that shows the amount taken out for federal taxes (along with any applicable State and City tax) from your salary ("earned") income. Banks and other investment institutions provide you with a "form 1099" (or sometimes a "form 1098") showing your taxable investment ("unearned") income. **Copies of all these forms are sent by your employer and investment institutions directly to IRS, to match against the copies you file with your return.**

"What" to file is a little more complicated. Most likely, if you are working you will get a "tax package" in the mail around January. It will provide you with a booklet of instructions and possibly with tax forms. If you are filing a paper tax form, you will need a form 1040, a 1040A or a 1040EZ.

When considering what form to use, remember that you pay taxes on *taxable* income, so your goal is to legitimately reduce this amount.

Many expenses, like charitable contributions, professional dues, some business trips, and child support are called "tax deductible," because they can be **subtracted** from your gross income. For example, let's say Dr. Richard Thanyou earns $10 million in a given year and donates $1 million to charity. The doctor's taxable income is now only $9 million, because the $1 million gift is tax deductible. If Dr. Thanyou were in the 50% tax bracket (that is, if the law required that half of all his taxable income would be paid as taxes), the savings would be 50% of $1 million, or $500,000 off his tax bill!! Of course, giving all of your money away only to reduce your taxes is self-defeating from a financial point of view, since you give away more than you save, but adding up all of your deductible expenses that arise in their own right during the year can reduce your tax bill **a lot**. And, from a non-tax point of view, it gives Dr. Jones an opportunity to give massively to a favored charity and be seen at the year's hottest charity party, while only costing $500,000. This maneuver is called "**itemizing deductions**." (Incidentally, the actual top tax bracket is lower than 50%; we'll discuss this later.) If your life is simple and a survey of legal deductions (see your tax booklet and tax form) reveals few that apply to you, you can claim a "**standardized deduction**." In a typical recent tax year this was $5,150 for a single taxpayer who is under 65 and not blind. The "standard deduction" is an amount considered fair by the government to cover money that you earned but gave away to charity or used for other specific deductible purposes designated by law, even though you do not choose to itemize. The rationale is that you shouldn't have to pay taxes on earned income disposed of in this manner.

Deductions, like charitable contributions, have been the subject of much discussion. There are pages and pages of deductions in the tax code. Clearly, they lower the amount of taxes paid and complicate the tax laws. So why are they there? Because Congress and the President use tax law to produce certain social or economic results not related to raising revenue. For example, most everyone thinks charitable organizations are a good thing; allowing a tax deduction helps convince people to support these groups by providing a financial incentive to do so. A simpler system, such as a "flat tax," would provide for few (or no) such social policy concepts, and therefore would be a more "neutral" tax. Whether that is a good idea, we leave to you.

What's so easy about the EZ?

You can usually file the 1040EZ if your taxable income is under $50,000, provided that (these are the most common requirements):

> you are single or married filing jointly

> you are not claiming any dependents

> you are under 65 and are not blind

> you had only wages, salaries, tips, unemployment compensation, and taxable scholarships or fellowship grants, and your taxable interest income was $400 or less

But, as always, there are some less common restrictions. Check it out.

The disadvantage to filing with this form, even if you qualify, is that you *cannot itemize deductions* (more about this later) or file as "head of household."

Still waiting for the EZ part? Well, everything's relative. It's easier than the 1040! And actually, in addition to being simpler, it has one other advantage—if you use the EZ one year, the next year you will probably be automatically sent information about filing by phone—we'll discuss this later.

The 1040 A also has specific requirements. Again, income must be under $50,000. You cannot itemize deductions, and the only allowed adjustment to your income is an IRA contribution (Chapter 3). There are also other restrictions on the source of your income (generally, it must come from wages, interest, taxable scholarships and grants, unemployment compensation and a few other areas) and on the types of credits you can apply to your taxes.

If these two forms don't fit, don't give you the best advantage (because, for example, you need to be able to itemize deductions), or you are not sure, then use the standard 1040.

What do I need to know to fill out the tax form?

Before starting on your return, assemble all your W-2s and 1099s for the tax year, along with all receipts you might need, such as charitable deductions, home mortgage payment information, and your checkbook register (the list of checks you maintain with your checkbook). You will also want a calculator and probably your favorite headache pill! By the way, the IRS estimates that filling out a standard 1040 tax form (including record keeping, learning about the law, preparing the form, assembling, and mailing the form) takes, on the average, about 10 hours, and that's without the special attachments that many taxpayers need. So don't start on the evening of April 14!!.

Let's take a look at the basic sections of the form 1040. There are many specialized forms which are used as attachments, but, mercifully, you won't need most of them, and may not need any of them.

Two notes before we begin:

First, the provisions of the tax code are very, very detailed and almost every section and every word has many qualifiers, limitations, and requirements. To repeat all of them here would make this a very difficult and tedious chapter, and in the final analysis most of them would not apply to you; and further, specific dollar ceilings can (and do) change from year to year. We have tried to point out areas that most likely apply to you as a young person starting out. In all cases, you should check further—by reading the tax booklet, calling or visiting the IRS, or consulting a tax guide or software.

Second, you will notice right at the beginning of the tax form, under the label, a line asking if you wish to donate $3 towards funding the Presidential Election Campaign. This provision is intended to decrease reliance on large campaign contributions. If you elect this donation, it will come out of whatever taxes you would owe anyway; in other words, it neither decreases your refund nor increases your tax due. So, it's strictly your vote whether to check the box.

1.Filing status

There are 100,002 people interested in your marital status: your mother, your Significant Other, and the 100,000 employees of the Internal Revenue Service. But to the IRS, the world is not divided just into "married" and "single"; the law defines four categories:

married filing separately
single
head of household
married filing jointly

Most of these terms are generally self-explanatory. "Head of household" means a person who has paid over half the cost of keeping a home for a qualifying person (such as a parent or child).

For most people, the lower you can go on this list (all else being equal), the lower your taxes.

2.Exemptions

Exemptions are, loosely speaking, the number of dependents you have—that is, the number of people (including yourself) that you support. For each such person, in a recent typical tax year, you are entitled to "exempt" (deduct) $2,650 from your income. (Remember I. Will Struggleon and Dr. Richard Thanyou from Chapter 1.) For most people, in addition to themselves, dependents could include a spouse and your children under 19 (age 24 if in school). However, what "support" means and who is entitled to be a dependent have specific definitions and criteria. If in doubt, check it out.

3.Income

Volumes have been written, and court calendars have been filled, seeking to define what is, and is not, income. For our purposes, income is generally the salary you receive from any jobs you held during the tax year, along with any *taxable* dividends or interest. This is one major area where taxpayers can give themselves an advantage—learning how to protect interest and dividends by making at least some portion non-taxable. All dividends, interest and other profits on traditional IRAs are tax exempt for the present and are not reported on your tax forms until retirement. (Never fear however; withdrawals from those IRAs that are tax exempt now are taxed later, upon retirement—but because your "tax bracket" is probably lower when you retire, you will pay less tax on this income.) However, two of the "new" IRAs, Educational IRAs and Roth IRAs, are **NOT** deductible when you make the contributions, but they are tax free, if you meet the qualifications, when you withdraw them. (These two IRAs are discussed in Chapter 3, and since they will not provide you with a tax break at the current time, we will not discuss them further in this chapter.)

Other income may also apply but would be atypical for someone starting out. If you received any income from any source, you need to determine its taxability.

4.Adjusted Gross Income (AGI)

When you become familiar with the term Adjusted Gross Income and have learned to think of it as AGI, you are ready to join the ranks of adults who like to talk about taxes and how to beat them. This is where you lower your taxable income by legally deducting (taking out) **certain income.** The advantage of this section is that deductions here are "above the line"; that is, **they reduce the income which becomes the adjusted gross income—and it is the adjusted gross income from which you subtract a standard deduction or itemized deductions.** *Thus, the lower you can make your adjusted gross income, the better your position will be for computation of your taxes.*

A major example that hopefully applies to you is your IRA contribution (Chapter 3). Recent tax law now permits many IRA contributions to be fully or partially tax deductible for certain individuals *even if they have a company retirement plan.* To qualify, in a recent typical tax year, you must earn below $40,000 (filing single) or $60,000 (filing jointly). Depending on how much below that income level you are, your contribution will be all or partly deductible. The qualifying amount will change slightly every year, so you need to recheck each year to be sure you meet the new qualifications.

A second new feature is the "spousal IRA" which permits a married couple to contribute up to $2000 to each of their IRA's, *without regard to which partner earned the income*. So, if you are married, and only one of you has an income, you can still place as much as $4000 in tax deductible IRAs, if you meet the qualifications. You may want to look into this option.

One particular deduction which might apply to you is moving expenses. If, for example, you have taken a job 50 miles or more from your old home, you may find that you are eligible to deduct certain moving expenses.

Another deduction which might apply is the Medical Savings Account (MSA). This new provision applies to some individuals who have had these special savings accounts established; generally they must be either self-employed or working in a business with fewer than 50 employees and have medical plans with high deductibles. If you feel you may qualify, speak to the Personnel Department at your job, and check your tax reference material. If you are self-employed, there is also a provision concerning health insurance, which may permit significant deductions. Again, if you think you may qualify, check it out.

If you pay alimony, there may be some relief for you in this section of the tax form. Because these provisions are so technical, you need to review them very carefully.

Of great interest are the provisions of the tax law that took effect in 1998. For example, **individuals who are repaying student loans (or are repaying student loans for a spouse or dependent), may be able to deduct a significant amount; while this amount varies from year to year, in 2001, for example, it is $2500.** If you think you may be eligible, be sure to check the tax booklet mailed with your tax forms. The loan must have been for qualified higher education expenses at an accredited institution. Note, however, that this deduction is phased out gradually as your income rises; so, taxpayers with adjusted gross income of under $40,000 ($60,000 if joint) can receive the full deduction, if eligible, but those with incomes between $40,000 and $50,000 (or $60,000 to $75,000 if joint) will receive only a portion of the benefit. Persons earning over these amounts cannot claim this benefit at all. But then, if your education helped you achieve that income, the money you spend repaying is well spent.

Remember: all of the deductions covered in this section lower your gross income to an "adjusted gross income."

5.Lowering your Adjusted Gross Income and Tax Computation

Once you have determined your AGI, the tax instructions will provide you with information on how to determine your actual tax due. It is here that you will apply your exemptions and, if you are claiming the standard deduction, your marital filing status.

Remember, the standard deduction is a flat amount which you can deduct from your AGI. (If you are single, the standard deduction for a recent year is $4,150; if married filing jointly, $6,900.) You may also choose to itemize deductions, but itemizing makes sense **only if your total itemized deductions are greater than the**

standard deduction. For example, certain expenses—some medical fees paid by you (not by your health plan), state taxes, real estate and property taxes, home mortgage interest, gifts to charity, and certain unreimbursed job expenses—can be subtracted ("claimed"). The new tax law also permits additional deductions for qualified long-term health care insurance and for unreimbursed expenses for the care of a chronically ill individual. *Look this section over carefully before you determine whether to take the standard or itemized deduction.*

This section drives much of what you see in our economy. Home purchases, charity benefit parties, business lunches, and other such staples of our society are fueled by the holy grail of the tax industry—the search for the itemized deduction. Party on!

At the end of this section, you compute the taxes due on your AGI, adjusted by deductions and exemptions, depending on your income: the tax table for income under $100,000 and the tax rate schedule for $100,000 or more.

6.Credits

A tax "credit" is not a deduction that reduces your AGI **but is far better—a direct reduction of your tax bill itself.** Assuming a tax bracket of 30%, Dr. Thanyou, earning $10,000,000/year, can lower his taxable income to $9,000,000 with a $1,000,000 charity contribution, saving $300,000 in taxes. **BUT, if the doctor had a *tax credit* of $1,000,000, the tax bill would actually drop by the full credit amount—$1,000,000.**

There are a few credits that may be directly subtracted from tax owed (which, of course, can be even better than subtracting deductions from your gross income). But they probably will not apply to you—the major ones are credit for child and dependent care, credit for the elderly or disabled, and credit for foreign taxes. One new credit (about $5000) is now allowed for adoption expenses; and for 1998, there is a dependent child credit of up to $400 for each dependent child under 17. If any of these sound like they might apply, get further information from the tax booklet, IRS, software, the tax guides, or a professional tax preparer.

Beginning in tax year 1998, there were some significant new educational tax credits, which could be useful, but only in very specific and limited circumstances. One is the **HOPE scholarship credit**. This provision allows a credit of up to $1,500 for qualifying educational expenses (tuition and related items) for persons enrolled in a post-high school undergraduate program—only for the first two years. Note, therefore, that *this credit cannot be used for graduate* **programs,** nor for the junior and senior years of college. The credit is reduced for income above $40,000 ($80,000 if joint) and is eliminated completely for income over $50,000 ($100,000 if joint). The credit also cannot be claimed if the student has made a tax-free withdrawal from an education IRA that year. The other is the **Lifetime Learning Credit, which can be applied to undergraduate, graduate and professional expenses** and thus may be more widely applicable. The maximum allowable amount is $1,000 per taxpayer return **and it can be used for an unlimited number of years, as long as the individual or dependents are enrolled. Although your time for taking advantage of the HOPE credit may be past, your younger siblings could benefit, so give them or your parents a call. The Lifetime Learning Credit may still apply to you.**

Note that for both these educational credits, the parent OR the child (but not both) may claim the credit.

7.Other Taxes

Some folks owe additional special taxes, like self-employment tax, household employment tax, social security and a Medicare tax on tip income not reported to employers. Again, if you work for a company and do not employ anyone yourself, you probably will not fall into this category, but give it a quick check to be sure.

8.Payments

Here you list payments that offset taxes due. Any tax already withheld ("withholding") from your salary by your employer during the year will, of course, be a major part of this offset.

In addition, although you may not be ready to play in the big leagues of itemized deductions, Congress has provided one benefit which may apply to you, called the Earned Income Credit (E.I.C.)—which, despite its name, falls into the payment section, rather than the credit section, of the form 1040! **The EIC is crafted to help low-income earners under specific circumstances.** In general, it applies to individuals with a modified AGI (oh dear, one more variation on income; for now consider it the same as AGI) under $25,760 **and** at least one "qualifying" child (that is, a dependent child) **OR** income under $9,770 without a "qualifying child." Other criteria you must meet include investment income under $2,250; not being a dependent on your parent's return; and, if you do **not** have a "qualifying child," you must be at least 25 years old, but under age 65. You must also have a Social Security Number. **The EIC reduces taxes you owe, and may give you a refund even if you don't owe any tax at all! But be warned: persons who knowingly and wrongly claim this credit may not be allowed to take the credit in future years.**

9.Refund/Amount Due

At last the bottom line: If taxes you owe are more than the payments (withholding) already made, you must pay the difference—with a check attached to your tax return. If the payments are more than the tax owed, you get a refund.

If the refund is very large, you have the option of decreasing your tax withheld during the current year. (But, as we explain in CHAPTER 10, a refund represents a kind of automatic savings account. Think carefully about the best strategy for you to achieve your investment goals—increasing your take-home pay by a relatively small amount each pay period may not be as productive as applying your tax refund to an IRA account.) Of course, if you owe a significant amount, you should increase your paycheck withholding. Your employer will give you a form W-4 to accomplish this.

There must be an easier way!

You can, of course, pay a professional tax preparer, and if you have really complicating factors affecting your taxes, that may be wise.

Another fairly new option is tax preparation software. This software will walk you step by step, asking questions about your specific situation, through completion of the tax form. There are currently three major software products on the market: TurboTax (basic version sells for about $35), Kiplinger Tax Cut (basic version, about $20), and Parsons' Personal Tax Edge (basic version, about $19). Deluxe versions can include CD format rather than disk, as well as the text of some tax regulations, etc. If your tax situation is relatively straightforward, the basic versions are probably sufficient.

Which software to buy? Consumer Reports (March 1997) tested all three, using a hypothetical taxpayer with a fairly complicated situation. Even under these circumstances, the three tested at least "good" in all areas (overall, question clarity, and presentation). Overall, TurboTax scored best, but also costs the most. One additional factor you may want to consider is whether the particular software you are considering can also do your state as well as federal tax.

Sources of assistance (most of them free):

For forms:

> Available at many public libraries and post offices as well as IRS offices (At some of these sites, in addition to hard copies, you can obtain a printout from a CD ROM or from the Internet.)
>
> Order by mail, using the coupon in your tax booklet.
>
> Request forms by phone (1 800 TAX FORM)
>
> Find them on your computer, at the IRS Web Site (http://www.irs.ustreas.gov).
>
> Request them by fax (703 368-9646)
>
> Obtain a CD ROM (call 202 512-1800). However this CD ROM is not free and should be used only if you really need a complete collection of all of IRS' 2000 strange and wonderful forms to impress your friends. If this collection does impress them, find new friends.
>
> Obtain computerized forms through tax preparation software that will permit you to enter the data onto the computer and

then print the forms for you. Be sure the software package has the 1040 PC logo, so you know that it is acceptable to the IRS.

For assistance in completing the form or understanding the law:

Dial Tele-tax, covering 150 specific topics. Your tax booklet lists phone numbers and topics.

Use the Website mentioned above for a variety of informational material.

Seek walk-in service at many IRS offices; call your local office to check sites and hours. In addition, your local office can also give you information about Volunteer Income Tax Assistance (VITA) folks who assist people with special needs (such as individuals with disabilities).

Special help is also available for those needing Braille versions. Also, for those with access to TTY/TDD equipment for the hearing impaired, call 1-800 829 4059 for assistance.

The form is complete. Now what?

Now you have several choices:

Mail the completed form with all attachments (W2 and other items you are instructed to attach) to the address listed in your tax booklet. Use either the U.S. Postal Service or a private delivery service (any of the standard ones will do—but it's even better to file sufficiently early that you don't need to pay for overnight delivery). Your return is considered timely filed if it is properly addressed, has sufficient postage, and is postmarked by the due date. A private company can provide you with proof of the posting date; the Post Office can provide you with proof if you use registered mail, but again, this costs extra—and if you file with a least a full day to spare, should not be necessary.

Also, remember that if you are mailing your return to an IRS Post Office box, private delivery services cannot deliver it; only the U.S. Postal Service can deliver to a postal box.

Telefile: Some taxpayers are eligible to file by phone (no paper!); if you are, you will be notified by mail. For example, if you used a form 1040EZ, you get information automatically on telefile next year. *You cannot file by this method unless you are contacted first by the IRS and told you are eligible.*

On-line filing through your computer: You can file your return using a personal computer equipped with a modem and IRS-accepted tax software. (Remember, earlier we indicated you could use software to enter and print your form; the electronic filing option is an additional service and will cost more.) The software allows you to file your return electronically for a fee through the software company. Tax preparation software (as described above) usually includes the ability to upload your completed electronic return to an on-line filing company which will, in turn, make your return compatible with IRS' requirements and send it on for filing. The IRS will notify this filing company, within 48 hours, whether the transmission was acceptable—and, of course, if there is a problem, the company will notify you. These companies charge a fee—generally in the $30 range—for filing your return electronically, but the fee is less when you file through a company whose tax preparation software you have used. For example, TurboTax's on-line company charge is about $10, and some companies may offer free software to certain low income taxpayers; you may want to check this out.

But, if you're approaching this project they same way you did your term papers, that is, doing it the night before the deadline, you should know that lots of other taxpayers have the same idea, and the on-line filing company may have a deadline several weeks sooner than the IRS. For example, to file using Turbo Tax, you may need to send your return to their on-line company by April 1, to give them sufficient time to forward it to IRS by April 15. Whichever on-line company you use, be sure that they are approved by the IRS. You can find a list of approved companies on the IRS web site at www.irs.ustreas.gov.

Electronic filing through a tax preparer: Many tax preparers will, for a fee, file your return electronically. If you use a tax preparer to file your return electronically for you, be sure they display a sign that indicates they are an IRS "authorized e-file provider" so that you know they are legitimate, and **check their fee first.**

If you file electronically, you receive an acknowledgment of filing within 48 hours; also, you may file early, and even if you owe tax may defer paying it until April 15. **The really big advantage for you in using an alternative to paper filing is that your refund comes much more quickly**: 16 days on the average for electronic filing, versus 38 for paper. However, you may pay for the privilege—so decide whether the speed of filing and receiving a refund is worth the fee for you.

Also, if you use any tax preparer service, be warned : Some preparers will offer you what appears to be an "instant refund" from them, instead of waiting for the actual IRS refund. **What they are really offering you** is a loan against that refund—but you will usually pay a hefty fee for this. If you can, wait for the actual refund.

If you use telefile, no paper documents need be submitted. It is truly a paperless process. However, if you file through other "paperless systems" some paperwork is, alas, required. If you filed by uploading from your personal computer, you still need to send your W-2s, (and any other supporting documents), and a signed signature document (Form 8453-OL) which your tax preparer or software package will provide. If you file electronically through a tax preparer, you will need to send the W-2s, supporting documents, and a form 8453. And, of course, either way, if you owe money, it will, unfortunately, still be necessary to pay—and this will mean sending in a check either at the time of filing or by April 15. Electronic filing is nice, but it deadens only some of the pain!

Some tips:

If you are lucky enough to deserve a refund, but haven't received it within three weeks, you can call the automated Teletax system for specific information about your refund status. The number to call will be in your tax booklet. Incidentally, if the IRS is late paying you the refund (generally, more than 45 days after the due date of the return), it will have to pay you interest!

If you aren't so lucky, and need to pay additional taxes, be sure to send a check, not cash. On the check include the tax year and the tax form you are filing (i.e., 1040, 1040A, etc.), along with your name (if not already pre-printed), telephone number, and social security number. Write the check out to the United States Treasury Department.

By the way, there is a provision in the new tax laws that will permit the IRS to accept certain tax payments by credit and debit card; whether this will apply to "ordinary taxpayers" we don't yet know. If it does, you could have another option for paying and, as we will see in Chapter 7, possibly for accruing some benefits.

IRS also offers the following suggestions to help prevent problems:

●Make sure all the social security numbers listed (you, spouse, dependents) are correct; the new tax law provisions permit the IRS to disallow a dependent if the social security number is missing or incorrect.

●Check your math.

●Sign and date the tax form, and enter your occupation.

●Use the peel off label included with your return. Some folks don't do this because they think the peel-off label contains "secret codes" which lead to being audited. They don't contain any such secret codes, but they do contain codes which will help the computer process your return quicker and get you your refund faster. If any information is incorrect, like your address and/or name, ink the correction right on the label. If you don't have a label, write the information in the space provided.

●If you have changed your name, be sure to notify the Social Security Administration before you file your return.

"Uh oh!"—

"Uh oh" #1: I don't have the money to pay!

If you have been following the steps outlined in this book (like preparing a budget and requesting enough withholding), you shouldn't be broke. But, if you are...don't despair, and don't put off filing your return past the due date. You can make arrangements to pay in monthly installments by filing a form 9465 (which you get by calling 1-800-829-3676). However, you will owe interest and possibly a late payment penalty as well as a fee. So this is not a good idea—the extra expenses add up rather quickly and alarmingly.

"Uh oh!" #2: I filed my return, but now I realize I made a mistake.

Perhaps you realized after you filed for this or a previous year that you had income you should have reported and you therefore owe additional taxes. Or, more happily, you did not claim deductions you were entitled to and should have received a refund, or a larger refund. All you need do is file an amended return (and of course, the government has a number for this form also; it's a 1040X). Generally, you have three years to file for a credit or refund, and you will receive interest on the amount owed.

All of this information is for folks who have to file. You said earlier in this chapter that "most of us have to pay." How do I know if I am one of the lucky ones who doesn't have to?

Actually, it's not very lucky. Usually it means that you have very little income. Generally speaking, if you are a young person (the nice thing about tax law is that anyone under 65 qualifies for this definition) and single, and your gross income is $6,800 or over, in a typical recent tax year, you have to file. Remember in Chapter 1, **we defined gross as your salary before all deductions.** Here it also includes any other income you received in the form of money, goods, property and services that are not tax exempt. If you are under 65 and married, your minimum income for filing is $12,200 in a typical recent tax year.

Of course, tax law is never quite this simple. For example, there are other rules for head of households, widow(ers) etc., so it always pays to check your tax package carefully before deciding what requirements actually apply to you.

There is also one other major exception that may apply. If you are receiving some financial support from your parents, they may be claiming you as a dependent on their return and different rules apply. If you are under 24 **and** a student (defined as an individual attending school full time for some part of each of five months during the past year—see what we meant about every word in the tax code having many qualifying words?), or simply under 19, and receive some financial support, you may be a dependent for tax purposes—check with your parents.

If you are being claimed as a dependent and you are single, under 65, and not blind, you must file if, in a recent typical tax year,

a) your unearned income (such as dividends rather than salary) was $1 or more and the total of that unearned income plus your earned income (such as a taxable scholarship) was over $650;

or

(b) your unearned income was $0 and your earned income was over $4,150.

Of course, sometimes you may actually want to file, even if you do not legally have to! For example, let's say you held a job with an annual salary of $26,000, but you left after only two weeks. You only earned $1000, but you had taxes withheld on those two weeks of salary, as if you were going to be earning your full annual salary. The only way to get that withholding back is to file a return, and show that you are entitled to a refund.

Okay, I've followed your instructions. I'm done!! Whew!

Not quite. That was the federal form. You'll need to follow a similar process for your state tax return, if applicable, and also for a city tax if applicable and not included in your state return. (New York City tax, thankfully, is included in a section of the New York State return.) If you lived in more than one State during the tax year, you may have to file more than one State return.

This can all be quite tedious. But understand: a significant portion of your money goes to taxes. In fact, the federal tax rate varies from 15% to as high as 39.6% of your salary. Typically, if you work a five day week, Monday you are working for the United States Government. (No wonder they call it Blue Monday!)

Gone But Not Forgotten

Once your return is mailed, you probably would like never to think about it again. Unfortunately, we can't guarantee that. First, you may possibly need to file an amended return and will need to see your original return plus attached documents. Second, on the scary side, you might be "audited"—this dreaded word means that the IRS has chosen your tax return for review. Audits can be random or more likely because some factor in your return appears out of the ordinary or in need of documentation. For example, perhaps you claimed unusually large charitable deductions. The audit process will require you to present proof that you did, in fact, make such contributions. Canceled checks or other receipts will suffice. If you cannot substantiate your claim, you may owe additional taxes.

Therefore, **keep all financial records,** including the tax return, attachments, canceled checks, receipts, credit card statements, etc. How long must you live surrounded by these mementos? The IRS advises you to keep them for three years from the date of filing or two years from the date the tax was paid, whichever is later. Of course, some records should kept longer, because they will be needed later. For example, records relating to home improvements may be needed years later when the home is sold. **And note that many knowledgeable C.P.A.'s advise that you keep your 1040's and IRA data forever!**

Well, that's it: now you know what you owe. We've already covered how to grow what you have, so hopefully, if you manage these two ends of your financial life well, you can update the saying we quoted at the beginning of this chapter: "nothing is certain **but wealth and taxes!**"

Chapter 6

The Backwards Budget: A Savings Plan that Works

Well, soon you'll be there—a job, a checking account, a good grip on taxes, ready for saving, investing, and an IRA—but no money leftover for this stuff!! Mom and Dad, your friendly banker, and other finance books would say that your problem is a budget—namely, that you don't have one. You can hear it now: "Get organized—just set aside what you need for food, shelter, transportation, clothes, recreation, utilities, etc., etc., etc., and after these are taken care of, save the rest"…*yeah right!*

PART I: SAVE FIRST, SPEND LATER

Well, Mom and Dad, the fact is that money in anybody's pocket is money spent, and the only way you can be sure to save for an IRA or for future big-ticket dream expenses (like a down payment on a car, or a great vacation, or furniture), is **to put away the cash before you ever see it.**

Most people new to the full-time working world have never heard of this concept, because it has no correlate in the pre-working life. After all, when your allowance was $5.00 a week you were given $5.00 to save or spend (i.e., *spend*) as you saw fit. Part-time work in high school or college was the same; $4.50/hour at Big Burgers or Bargain City gave you a paycheck that you saved or **spent** (i.e., spent); no one ever told you to save money before you had it. How could you!?

So how does it work?

The concept to remember is: PAY YOURSELF FIRST!! WE REPEAT—PAY YOURSELF FIRST, NOT LAST, BUT FIRST. Put away a certain amount of cash, depending on your goals and income, before you see any spendable money. You can't easily spend it, if you don't really have it around.

Plan A:

Your employer's payroll department may offer a "payroll savings plan." A payroll savings plan allows you to designate a portion of your paycheck for direct deposit into a bank or credit union; you never "see" this money before it is deposited. (A payroll saving plan should not be confused with routine "direct deposit" of your salary—in which your paycheck is deposited electronically into your checking account, or with an "automatic investment plan," which automatically deducts a specified amount from your checking account each month.) A payroll savings plan and direct deposit are not mutually exclusive; in fact, you can have both operating simultaneously (and you probably should).

Sounds good…but my employer never heard of a "payroll savings plan." Am I out of luck?

Plan B:

If your employer has no payroll savings plan, you can use the government-mandated automatic withholding mechanism to be sure that more taxes are taken out of your paycheck than your income and number of dependents would justify (CHAPTER 1, CHAPTER 5, CHAPTER 10), in which case you will receive a prompt refund after you file your tax return, which you use to start your IRA or investment plan!

Conventional finance books and financial advisors hate this approach, because for the entire year the State and Federal Governments have your money on deposit and collect interest on it, whereas if you had the money it would be working for you, collecting interest or growing in value as an investment. BUT—they assume that you would save or invest the money if you had it—a dubious proposition, in our view.

In CHAPTER 10, Putting it All Together, we describe, step-by-step, a practical strategy for using a payroll savings plan or the automatic withholding mechanism to (1) establish an IRA and (2) begin a savings/investment program that is accessible for big-ticket dream items.

PART II: SPENDING WHAT'S LEFT

People without any budget tend to spend as they go, and if they go a lot—to the movies, to restaurants, to concerts—they have nothing left when bills come in for the non-fun stuff, like rent. The adult approach to this problem is called a budget.

The traditional way to proceed with a budget is to make a list of all of your "fixed" expenses, like rent or college loan repayments, and deduct these from your take-home pay. The balance (if any) represents your **discretionary income**—money no one else has any claim to, so you can use it according to your discretion, for eating out, movies, clothes, CD's, and so on. Savings are left for the very end, so guess what? Nobody (or almost nobody) saves. Living from check-to-check has become virtually a national pastime.

Unfortunately, most everyone has to have a budget of some sort, and so do institutions—your college, your company, and your country. They all make their lists of non-discretionary items and try to parcel out what remains. In practice, for an individual this exercise is hard, *really hard*, because the meager remaining discretionary funds never seem to cover the things you **really want and, frankly, don't think of as discretionary**—like having a little fun on the weekend. Colleges get around this by fundraising among alumni, as you will soon discover; companies can issue bonds, and the government has a special advantage—it can run at a deficit, that is, it can print bonds and sell them to finance projects that can't be paid for out of income!! (Does this sound a little like official counterfeiting?)

You will receive many tempting offers to do the same and live beyond your means (CHAPTER 7, Credit Cards), charging whatever you want, racking up huge credit card debt, paying the minimum each month, and owing gigantic interest in only a few months. But, unlike large companies, colleges, or the government, you do not have many financing options. So, we advise avoiding credit cards for the first six months after graduation, and we regretfully join in the chorus of people advising you to set up a budget and live within in it.

However, this need not be as grim as it sounds. Continuing with our approach to "the backwards budget", we urge you to take stock of what is really discretionary and non-discretionary for you, in terms of what adds the greatest comfort and pleasure to your daily life. Try to factor these items into your budget as if they were "fixed expenses", like rent. A budget is like a diet for your wallet, and you can stick with a diet much better if it includes a few of your favorite treats. *So, budget, yes; starvation, no.*

First, deduct from your take-home pay whatever truly mandatory expenses you have—for example, rent, utilities (heat, electricity, basic phone service), and loan repayments. Then, make a list of all your living expenses, including the essentials like basic food costs, and the things that are *really important,* but not strictly speaking "essential", like going out with your friends. *Realistically* estimate what these expenses would be in a typical month. If you have either a very comfortable salary or very Spartan tastes, you may find that your expenses fit well within your remaining take-home pay; if so, since your savings have already been taken care of, you can skip the rest of this chapter!

More likely, you will find your estimated expenses greatly exceed your take home pay (ours do!). Now, rank the items on your list in terms of their importance to you and how much of your income you are willing to devote to them. Keep refining this list until the amount fits within your take home pay. Working from this amount, test these figures against reality for one month. You may find, for example, that you have ranked your living quarters as relatively unimportant compared to clothes, and you want to spend less on rent. Consider your options—if an apartment is relatively unimportant to you, sharing an apartment, or renting a room in some one's home may be sufficient; or, perhaps you can reduce your rent further by offering to help in apartment upkeep by shoveling snow, raking, etc. Initially, you may even prefer to live with your parents (gasp!!), paying them only a small sum to cover additional expenses you cause.

The point is, shape the budget by the way you want to live, making the most sacrifices in the areas least important to you. Do not be swayed by conventional thinking, for example that living with parents at first is *always* a bad idea or that living outside of Manhattan just isn't cool for a New Yorker. **That way, your budget, although undoubtedly still difficult to follow, will at least provide some day-to-day satisfactions in the areas that make you feel best.**

And remember, your savings are happening automatically, as we explain step-by-step in CHAPTER 10 (Putting it All Together), so, if you have "nothing" left over at the end of the month, your financial worth is nevertheless growing. And, if some unexpected money comes your way—perhaps a birthday gift or a bonus at work—you can indulge yourself on luxury without guilt.

Chapter 7

Credit Cards—the Good, the Bad, and the Ugly

If a total stranger walked up to you on the street and asked to borrow $1000, you'd need a lot of convincing before you would agree. And yet, amazingly, hard-boiled financial professionals in the credit card business will be begging for the privilege of advancing you large sums of money—that is, letting you borrow like mad—*with very few questions asked*! There must be a catch…

There is. Ever hear of Catch 22? Well, in the credit card business, it's Catch 16, or 17, or even 18—that's the interest rate that these companies may charge for the money they lend you, and make no mistake about it—when you use a credit card, you are borrowing money and the company is lending, *no two ways about it*! So, before you even think about diving headlong into the world of plastic, ask yourself this question: "Do I want to start out in life borrowing more money? Before contracting plasticmania, inoculate yourself with some information on what to avoid.

First, some basics: "debit card" versus," credit card":

Earlier (CHAPTER 4) we talked about checking accounts and debit cards. **A debit** card does **not** advance you any credit—that is, you can't spend more than you have in your bank checking account (and its over-draft protection, if you have it). It is really just a plastic, reusable check; any time you use it the amount spent is deducted from your checking account. As long as you are careful to subtract the amount spent on each debit card purchase from your check register as soon as you get home, debit cards can be extremely helpful, especially because many banks allow a large number (sometimes an unlimited number) of debit card transactions per month, free or for a minimal fee, so you can use your limited number of free checks for payments like rent and avoid repeated ATM cash withdrawals and their high fees. When you are just starting out and are not certain of your ability to withstand temptation, this is the way to go. You may get some icy stares when your transaction can't go through because your checking account is down to zero, but you won't experience the numbing chill of going below zero—i.e., getting a credit card "statement" (bill) at the end of the month, only to find that you have charged more than you can pay.

Credit cards, on the other hand, offer you little protection against excessive debt. When you apply for the card, the company will ask for some basic information, including your salary. Based on this information it will offer you a "line of credit"—often several thousand dollars. In other words, you can keep charging stuff on your card until you reach that limit. If your friendly card company has granted a credit line of $2000, you could go out immediately and buy $800 worth of stereo equipment, and $1200 worth of other stuff! Party time, big time, right? *Not quite*: the stores where you charged the stuff will send their bills to the credit card company, and the credit card company will pay them; then, at the end of the month, it will collect all the charges it has paid for you and send you the bill. The card company, in effect, is "trusting" you to find $2,000 and pay it back, usually within two weeks. (Incidentally, the card company charges each store a small fee, usually less than 1% of the purchase price of each item charged; when you ponder the dollar volume of goods charged world-wide, you can easily appreciate why profit margins of banks and finance companies are so bloated.)

The problem for the card user is that along the way, when you were charging up a storm, there was no signal of any kind that you were exceeding your ability to repay; you receive no "real time" or "running total" of your accumulating credit card debt, unless you reach your $2000 credit limit. Why? **Because the credit card company does not want you to have the money to pay its full bill.** They want you to pay just a little bit of that $2000 (called "the monthly minimum," which can be $50 or even less) *and to owe them the rest—i.e., they lend you the unpaid balance.* So, as you might expect, millions and millions of Americans get in over their heads and pay only the monthly minimum on each credit card bill. So far, so good, right? This is really cool…I can charge a lot and pay a little… *Not really*…the company adds a hefty monthly finance charge to the amount you haven't paid. And that's the catch we described—the 16% (or more) interest you will pay for this "loan".

Is this really so bad? No, not really, it is not "so bad," it is totally awful! What does "16% interest" actually mean? The interest rate is usually described as the "APR," meaning 16% Annual Percentage Rate—that is, they are charging you 16% per year for the loan. We have seen in CHAPTER 3 how interest compounded over the years can perform miracles for your IRA—Baron Rothschild once called compound interest the eighth wonder of the world—well compound interest working against you is just as powerful. For example, a $2000 balance "carried over" from month to month for five years would result in over $1000 in interest charges alone—and of course you would still owe the original $2000 for stuff you bought! The only way to avoid this snare is to pay off the full amount on your monthly credit card bill. In fact, this method turns the tables on credit card companies, because they have lent you the money until you pay the bill for goods you have charged, and yet they receive no interest when the bill is paid in full! (If everybody did this, the card companies would probably go belly-up.) And, if you have a card that gives you special "extras," like a small cash rebate or frequent flyer miles, **you do not forfeit these perks when you pay the bill in full.** By being careful and smart, you can actually come out not just even, but ahead!

We admit that credit cards have many advantages. For example, they make it possible to purchase by phone, mail, or internet. And some activities would be very difficult without a card; for example, it is difficult to rent a hotel room without a card (having your card on record protects the hotel against your walking out in the morning without paying), and it is virtually impossible to rent a car without a credit card, because a small cash deposit would hardly be compensation to the company if you drove off with the car and never returned. If you are traveling abroad, credit cards let you withdraw money from local banks, in the local currency, so you need not guess how much money to take along, and you don't need Travelers Checks. Credit cards are also great in emergencies—if your car breaks down far from home, how else will you pay for repairs?

Cards have other practical benefits. Monthly statements provide a record of purchases, handy in reviewing your spending habits to figure out where your money goes. You may not realize that some buyer protection comes with a credit card; the Fair Credit Billing Act gives you certain important rights. If the item you buy is defective, for example, and you have made a good faith effort to resolve the problem, you may *legally* withhold payment for the item. There are some limitations; if the card used was not a card issued by the store where you bought the item, or if the card is a "travel and entertainment card" (like Diner's Club and American Express), then you must meet two requirements for this protection: the purchase must have cost more than $50, and the purchase must have taken place in the state where you live, or within 100 miles of your home.

There are few major credit card "brands": the overwhelming number are VISA, Master Card, American Express, Diner's Club, and Discover. However, there are countless issuers of these cards, and some department stores (like Neiman Marcus) have their own "exclusive cards"; the issuers individually define the conditions (cost of card, interest charged on unpaid balances) that govern the card's use.

Everyone who works—even I. Will Struggleon—gets many unsolicited credit card offers. (In a recent three-year period, Americans received a total of 8 billion credit card offers, according to the New York Times!) So companies have developed numerous enticing approaches to beat the competition. Depending upon the gimmicks and associated conditions, these cards can be good, bad, or downright ugly.

The personal approach—the "affinity card":

Some companies target your specific background or identity. The card may be connected to your college or a favorite charity; the credit card company gives them a *very small* share of its profits. So, each time you charge something you feed the homeless or help your *alma mater*. Or, they may target your professional group and appeal to your pride in displaying that membership every time you charge something (the card will have, for example, a college logo). Imagine yourself with a Yale University VISA, at your favorite cigar bar, charging brandy and a couple of Havana Specials…that'll knock their socks (or pantyhose, as the case may be) off!

These kinds of cards usually fall into the Ugly category: they have annual fees that you pay for the privilege of owning one, above and beyond any interest on unpaid balances carried over from month to month, and their APRs are no bargain. Our advice: if you want to support your college or a charity, make a direct contribution. You and the institution will come out ahead. If you want to advertise your membership in an organization, get a bumper sticker, ring, logo tie, or nose plug, not a credit card.

The introductory low percentage rate:

Among the Ugly cards, this advertising technique is common. You receive a brochure in the mail promising a low rate (APR) of only 5.9%. Now we don't recommend paying **any** finance charges on credit cards, but clearly 5.9% *is* better than 16%, so what's the problem? The problem is that this low rate lasts only a few months, after which the rate zooms to double digits. The company counts on the likelihood that you will have carried over enough charges, suckered in by this low rate, that in a few months, when the rate soars, you will be hit with major finance charges.

Here's the actual fine print of one card that came in an envelope announcing a 7.9% APR:

> The APR for cash advances is 16.5%. The APRs may vary and are determined by adding 7.9% to the Prime Rate (PR) for purchases and for Cash Advances...If this account is not in good standing during any portion of the 12 month period prior to the billing period ("review period") you will be assessed interest at PR+12.9%, currently 21.15%, for purchases and for cash advances and you will forfeit the introductory rate.

In other words, if you get caught owing them money, because you didn't pay even the monthly minimum—a real possibility in this uncertain world, where layoffs and downsizing are rife—you lose not only the 7.9% rate, you don't even get the prime rate (the rate financial institutions charge their best customers, usually other financial institutions), or even the regular customer rate of 16.15%. Your interest rate engages warp drive to **21.15%**. This goes *way beyond* Ugly; it makes a Klingon look cute. Forget-about-it!

Annual fee cards:

Some companies charge an annual fee for owning their card, **even if you don't ever use it**, ranging from $15 to more than $40. This fee does not necessarily make a card Ugly, but it does require some careful consideration. Often a card with an annual fee is sold as a "special," with its annual fee waived. First, be clear about whether the annual fee is waived for just the first year or is permanently obliterated. If the waiver is for one year only, and the card offers no other special advantage, skip it. (Chances are, you won't remember to switch to another equivalent card before the year is up, and you will be paying a fee for nothing.) But annual fee cards are not necessarily all bad; some of them offer special advantages, like "points" or "frequent flyer miles," in which case the fee can more than pay for itself. Read on.

Travel and Entertainment Cards:

Way back when, these were the dominant form of credit card! Strictly speaking, there is little credit involved. These cards traditionally required full payment each month; the credit was extended only from the time of purchase until the bill was due. You could not carry over any unpaid balance to the next month. Examples of these cards are Diner's Club and American Express (which now also has a "regular" card that permits carrying over balances to the next month). Are these cards good for you? *Well, if you can't trust yourself and are afraid of piling up debt, these cards are your ticket,* although you will pay a higher annual fee than for other credit cards. Although a few merchants will accept only this type of card, and some will not accept it at all, most will accept Master Card, VISA, and Travel/Entertainment cards.

The "precious metal" card:

"Precious metal" is not their official name, of course. However, many bank card issuers have introduced up-scale versions of their card with fancy names like "gold" or "platinum." These cost more than regular cards but serve the same basic purpose. Therefore, the companies will try to entice you through offering many "perks," like access to travel planning services. Think carefully before you decide on such a card, and don't fall for the supposed prestige; the truth is that people may care what color your money is, but they couldn't care less what color your card is. Decide instead if the benefits are really ones you need, and if they justify the annual fee.

Cards with Insurance:

Many cards offer all kinds of insurance benefits that you very likely do not need, but for which you are asked to pay dearly. For example, many offers include insurance in case you cannot make your monthly payments, for certain **specific, very limited** reasons. You may think from the brochure that this coverage is included with the card, but, in fact, it costs extra—typically between 50 to 80 cents, with variation from state to state, for every $100 you charge. The expense adds up quickly. The restrictive terms and conditions usually appear in paragraphs of very fine print. Here is a sample of just a few lines from one "explanatory statement" —actual print size reproduced here:

To be eligible for disability coverage, you must be gainfully employed 30 hours per week at the time your claim begins except in CA, GA, ID, IN, MD, MI, MO, NM, OK, TN, TX & WA. (Unemployment benefits are not available in HI, ME, MN & VT.) Unemployment must be involuntary and does not cover retirement, resignation, incarceration, periods in which you are paid for work previously done, or self employed people unless the business is closed for financial reasons.

In terms of unemployment benefits, keep in mind that if your company wants to fire you for cause, you may choose to resign, rather than have your employment record marred, and, in the case of this particular card, you will not be able to claim the benefit. Generally speaking we would characterize cards with these "benefits" as Bad.

The "secured" card:

This product is for people with very poor credit rating (perhaps due to bankruptcy or other problems) or no ability to resist temptation. A "secured card" **is not a credit card, because no real "credit" is involved,** although it looks and feels like one. You deposit a set amount of cash, say $500, in the company's bank; little, if any, interest is paid, and the card may also charge an annual fee. You are then allowed to charge up to the limit that you have already deposited, which must be paid by you before you can charge more. Since the company has your money in advance, it takes no risk; in fact, as your "charges" accumulate on the card, equivalent amounts in your secured card account at the bank are frozen as protection for the company. There is no particular advantage to you, because you have, in effect, paid for your purchases in advance. You might as well save the cash in your own bank and pay for purchases in cash, or, if you are seduced by the lure of plastic, use a debit card, which also gives you access to your money via checks.

In your situation, we see no need for this type of card and cannot recommend it.

The automatic trade down:

You will very often be offered a top-of-the-line card, with the largest credit line, lowest fees, and greatest benefits, but alas, in fine print, you find that if you don't qualify for this card, your application will **automatically** be transferred to a different card—one with fewer benefits and more charges! Again, take a look at some actual words from a brochure:

> In the event that I do not qualify under the terms and conditions described in this brochure, you may consider my application and all information contained in it to be an application for a card with different terms and conditions (italics added by us). This alternative card has different costs associated with it.

Incredibly, this wording is not even on the application but appears elsewhere in the brochure! When the actual card comes, you may not notice the difference until you see unexpected charges on the monthly statement. Trade-down trickery is very ugly!!

So, after all of this negativity, is the only good credit card no credit card?

Not necessarily, there are Good cards around.

A credit card provides you with a very convenient record of your purchases. It allows you to pay one bill each month, using only one check, instead of paying many separately. It offers advantages compared to cash, because you have protection against theft. Generally, you are not responsible for more than a specific, limited amount of charges ($50) if your card is lost or somehow used by an unauthorized person. **And a customer with a good credit rating who promptly reports a stolen card will usually not be charged for any purchases charged by the thief.** Also, in a dispute over the correctness of a charge by a merchant—i.e., if you think you have been cheated, charged too much—the credit card company will in some cases **represent you** in disputing the charge! Also, if you have questions at any time about any item on your monthly statement, we have found that credit card "hot lines" are always open and usually very knowledgeable about billing processes, dispute adjudication, and the entire system.

In general, we recommend against a credit card for the first six months that you are on your own. You are adjusting to rent, perhaps repaying a car and/or college loan, making IRA deposits, paying taxes, and settling into a new job. Enough is enough. A credit card can be just one hassle too many.

However, as we have said, there are many practical reasons why a credit card is useful, and, in fact, most new graduates have already succumbed to the call of plastic. But whether you are already a card-holder or not, think about the different types of cards. If there is no particular feature, like frequent flyer miles (see below) that really makes sense, then base your choice on cost, primarily the **ANNUAL PERCENTAGE RATE**, the yearly interest charge, as a percentage of the dollar amount you carry over from one month to another. Many more subtle factors figure into credit card cost, usually ignored even by responsible users with an excellent credit rating. If details are your passion, see appendix II for a daunting list.

Next, once you have selected a card, get the benefits without suffering big-time: (1) Charge only what you need or want so badly that it's part of your "essential expenses" (CHAPTER 6, PART II: SPENDING

WHAT'S LEFT). (2) When you charge something, you receive a slim receipt, chock full of information—date and time of transaction, location of transaction, price of item, tax, total charge, type of card used (e.g., MasterCard or VISA), your name, and the card number. **Save each and every receipt**, and each evening put them in a specific envelope. At the end of each week, **total up the week's charges**, and write these on the outside of the envelope, so you have a "running total" of your credit card debt. If you are getting in over your head—that is, if you are charging more than you will be able to pay IN FULL at the end of the month, leave your card at home, until that month's credit card bill is fully paid. You can't charge anything, let alone charge recklessly, if your card is in the bureau drawer, covered by two pairs of socks.

Now, if you feel that you can handle a credit card responsibly, read the offers you get carefully and consider getting **one** credit card. **Limit yourself to one**; the temptation of multiple credit lines can be too overwhelming for anyone. Read brochures carefully, now that you know what to avoid. Stay away from gimmicks and benefits that cost extra. Reject those with an annual fee, unless the card gives you something back that is more than worth the fee. **If you are a congenital 'debt junkie' but really need a card, resort to a travel/entertainment card that requires full payment at the end of each month. The hefty annual fee can be seen as "insurance"** against racking up excessive debt.

Cards that earn points: The good guys.

Some cards earn "points" with each purchase charged. These points give you specific bonuses. Discover, for example, actually sends a cash rebate, based on a percentage of the amount that you charged during the year. If you charged purchases of $3000 in a year, then at the typical rate of 1%, you will get a rebate of $30. That's not a lot, but it's better than nothing. Why not let the card company pay you, instead of your paying them?

With other cards, your purchase dollars accumulate points towards free airline tickets. While superficially appealing, these cards usually do not apply to the beginner, because you get 1 to 1.5 "dividend miles" per dollar charged, and it takes a lot of "dividend miles" to get a free ticket (for example, USAirways, whose "dividend miles" never expire—that's good!—requires 25,000 dividend miles for one coach class round-trip ticket within the continental United States and Canada). This does not mean that you can *fly 25,000 air miles*; it means that you have to have charged items worth $25,000 to get this one free round-trip ticket! (For the parent, this is a super deal, because many colleges accept VISA for tuition payments; so after a few kids have finished college, mom and dad get free tickets to their dream vacation—only problem is that after educating the brood they have no money to spend when they get there!)

For a recent graduate free airline tickets via credit card are a long way off, with one exception: if your job entails a lot of air travel, reimbursed by your company, one of these cards is a must, because the trips themselves accumulate credit towards free tickets—via "frequent flyer miles"—and if you charge your airline tickets on a card that accumulates "dividend miles," you accumulate even more credit towards free tickets because of the charge itself. Also, many cards that offer miles towards free tickets add "bonus miles" when you charge air tickets. **Bottom line**: if you travel a lot for your company, get this type of credit card; charge all of your trips on the card, and soon you'll be flying high (and free!).

Some cards accumulate points that can be applied to reduce the price of a new car. Although the offer is seductive, will you really be buying a new car? If a **new** car is not in the picture for a few years, make sure the credit you accumulate towards the purchase has no expiration date. GM still offers this type of card, but Ford has cancelled its car card program.

O.K., I've made my selection. I am using it responsibly. Anything else I need to know?

Of course! With something as powerful as a credit card (and make no mistake, the buying power of these cards is awesome) you have to exercise good judgment.

First, keep your card secure. Be aware of where it is, so you will know at once if it is lost. Be sure you have a record of *the card number and the phone number of the issuer.* (The account number and the phone number will be on your credit card statement). However, if you have a card you don't use much, you may not have a statement to refer to, so keep the material you were given when the card was issued. In a secure place (not where you keep your card) make a file with this data. **THE CARD NUMBER MUST REMAIN CONFIDENTIAL.** Keeping "the card secure" doesn't mean just *the physical card*; Don't let other people see your card. Carefully dispose of carbons or receipts that have the card number on them, because they could be used to charge items—on your account—by phone. If you are charging with the card by phone, be careful who is within earshot. Remember, the Truth in Lending Act protects you if your card is lost—you can't be held responsible for more than $50 of fraudulent charges. But, under the Act, *you can't be held responsible for any unauthorized charges after you report the loss, so call in a loss at once.* You may receive offers from companies that will, for an annual fee, keep a record of all your charge cards for you and then notify all the card issuers for you, if they are lost. However, if you keep records so that you can notify issuers promptly, there should be no reason to pay for this service.

Second, check your bill **each month**. Sometimes charges appear that are erroneous or unauthorized. Promptly follow up: call the company. The charges could be simple mistakes which the company will promptly correct, or the charges could indicate that your card has been compromised—someone unauthorized has access to, and is using, your card. After you have used a card for a while, and established your credit worthiness, credit card companies will establish a "profile" for your spending patterns and may even contact you to check out what appears to be an unusual pattern of charging! But don't rely on them; review the bill yourself. (See Appendix III for an excruciating list.)

What if you find an error? Once again the Fair Credit Billing Act comes to your rescue, by setting out a specific and mandatory procedure that companies (and you) must follow: Believe it or not, in this age of phones and e-mail, you must usually notify the company in writing, if your initial call is unsuccessful. The notification must be within 60 days of the mailing of the first erroneous bill. Include all necessary information (your name, account number, the error—date, amount, etc.—and why you believe it is wrong). Be sure to send the letter to the correct address—which may not be the same as the address for payments. Look on the statement to see where to send the letter, or check with customer service by phone.

Meanwhile, pay all other amounts which you are not disputing. The creditor must respond in writing within 30 days. And within 90 days (or two billing cycles, if that is sooner) the creditor must either correct the account or tell you why no correction is needed. If you are right, then, of course, the overcharge and any interest is canceled. If the creditor is correct, you will owe the amount along with interest.

When you maintain good security over your card, pay your charges promptly, and report misuse (or loss) of your card, you are building a good credit record, and in the next chapter we will see why that is so important.

By the way, credit card companies don't like people who use no-annual-fee cards and never incur finance charges. In the bizarre world of finance, such consumers, who pay all their bills on time and don't add to the company's profits, are considered bad—deadbeats! We think that kind of "deadbeat" is very smart and very good—not ugly at all. Try it!

APPENDIX I:
CARD COSTS FOR THE DETAILS FAN

●**Grace Period:** the amount of time, *variable card to card,* that a company will allow to elapse before charging interest on your purchases; obviously, the length of the charge-free interval affects your costs.

●**Minimum Payment:** the lowest amount that you can pay each month if you have a balance remaining ("outstanding"). For example, whether you owe $200 or $2000, the company may require that you pay **at least $50** (the minimum payment) and allow the rest to be carried over to the next month.

●**Interest Computation Method:** companies can vary in how they compute your interest. It can be calculated by the month or by the day. Let's say you carry over $100 in unpaid purchases, and you owe $2 in interest as a result. The next month your balance is $102, and interest is charged on the original purchase amount ($100) as well as on the interest ($2). Yup—you are paying interest on interest!

●**Outstanding Balance Computation Method:** *DO NOT purchase a card that uses this technique!* It means that if you owe any amount and carry it over to the next month, any purchases that you make next month begin to accrue interest immediately. In other words, you carry over $200 and interest accrues on the $200; so far, so good. But next month, you purchase goods for $100, and immediately, before you are billed, interest accrues on this $100 also, so you will see interest charges on $200, plus $100, or $300, on that month's statement.

●The Truth in Lending Act requires credit card companies to tell you up front and in plain language (well, relatively plain) what the costs of credit are. But it is up to you to read the material, understand it, and make an informed choice.

APPENDIX II:
How to Read and Interpret your Credit Card Statement

First, you should realize that the format and layout of credit card state-
ments is variable; many are clear, virtually self-explanatory. Some can
confuse you to the point of desperation. DO NOT HESITATE TO CALL
THE HELP NUMBER FOR HELP—THERE IS NO CHARGE FOR
THIS SERVICE, EVER, AND THE STAFF IS ALMOST ALWAYS
POLITE, KNOWLEAGEABLE, AND CLEAR.

Reproduced is the bottom part of a typical statement.

Account #: 000-000-000-000   Name: I. Will Struggleon

New Balance	Total Credit Available	Credit	Statement Closing Date	Minimum Payment Due	Payment Due Date
$ 400.25	$500.00	$99.75	1/31/00	$10.00	2/14/00

● "New Balance" refers to how much money you owe as of the
"closing date" of the statement.

● "Total Credit" indicates how much you could charge if you were
paid-up-in-full.

● "Credit available" tells you how much more stuff you can
charge, as of the "closing date," before you bump into your "credit

limit"—that is, the point where your card will not be approved by a seller. In this case, Will Struggleon's credit is $500, and he has charged $400.25 worth of stuff, so he has $99.75 to go, as of 1/31/00, before hitting his ceiling.

● "Minimum Payment Due" is the most seductive and worrisome part of the statement, let alone of the whole credit-card process. It means that you can get away with paying only this small sum— $10 in Will's case—and the remainder owed, $390.25, will simply appear on next month's statement as a "charge carried over," or "unpaid previous balance," with interest added, at the card's annual percentage rate.

> **DO NOT, REPEAT—*DO NOT*, FALL INTO THE HABIT OF PAYING THE MINIMIUM PAYMENT DUE. PAY ALL OR AS MUCH AS YOU CAN OF THE NEW BALANCE.** The best way to avoid the pitfall of routinely paying the "minimum payment due" is to never start

Wow! O.K., O.K. I get the point…But what's all that stuff in columns under "Transaction Summary"?

TRANSACTION SUMMARY

Transaction Date	Posting Date	Description	Reference Number	Amount
1/2/00	1/4/00	CD's, Music City.com	00000-0000-0000	$26.00
1/6/00	1/9/00	Shoes, Feet Galore	0000000-00—000	$74.00
1/10/00	1/13/00	Shoes, Feet Galore	0000000-00-000	CR $74.00
1/14/00	1/15/00	Furniture Town, Computer Desk	00000-00-00000	$374.25

This part of the statement is extremely helpful. As you can see, each "transaction" refers to a purchase that you made (or sometimes a return). On 1/2/00, Will bought CD's at Music City.com, charging $26 to his card. On 1/6/00 he bought running shoes at Feet Galore, for $74; but, on 1/10/00 he returned those shoes (they didn't fit) and his credit card account received a credit (CR) of $74. Will's big purchase of $374.25, at Furniture Town, plus the CD purchase of $26, accounts for his total "Current Balance": $400.25. By the way, "posting date" is simply the date that your transaction is recorded on the company's computer for inclusion in the current statement.

The shoes didn't fit, so Will took them back. What if the computer desk from Furniture Town is defective, and when he calls the store he gets the run around?

Here is where using a credit card for purchases can be very handy. Call the help line. Have your statement in front of you and be ready with your card number, expiration date, and address. Tell the card representative which transaction is the problem, and explain what the problem is. The card representative often will have the merchant's number available and may well call for you, or he/she may also ask you to write a note to the store, with the complaint, and a copy of the sales slip; if you receive no satisfaction within 30 days, call the help line again. Incredibly, the card company should then deal with the merchant for you, and arrange for the charge to be canceled and the item to be picked up. Bottom line: ask for help. You deserve it and will probably get it.

APPENDIX III:
an error is an error is an error, right? Not really...

If reviewing your bill in excruciating detail is your form of recreation, follow the Federal Reserve guidelines, a good summary of the provision of the Fair Credit Reporting Act, that defines a billing error as:

● a charge for something you didn't buy or for a purchase made by someone not authorized to use your account

● a charge that is not properly identified on your bill or is for an amount different from the actual purchase price or was entered on a date different from the purchase date; or

● a charge for something you did not accept on delivery, or that was not delivered according to agreement

● an error in arithmetic

● failure to show a payment or other credit to your account

● failure to mail the bill to your current address, if you told the creditor about an address change at least 20 days before the end of the billing period; or

● a questionable item, or an item for which you need more information.

Here are some other items the Federal Reserve advises you to look for:

●the date on the postmark. If your account is one on which no finance or other charge is added before a certain due date, then creditors must mail their statements at least 14 days before payment is due.

●the payment date entered on the statement. Creditors must enter payments on the day they arrive, so long as you pay according to instructions (sending your payment to the address indicated on your bill).

●any credit balances on your statement. Credits appear when you return a purchase, or somehow pay more that the total payment due on the statement. If you have a credit due, the credit card company must make a refund to you, or apply it to your next monthly bill. The refund must be made within seven business days after your written request, or automatically if the credit balance remains after six months. (In other words let's say that after you have earned a credit you stop using your card. After six months, the company must stop waiting for a charge to apply the credit against, and must issue the refund, by mail, to you).

Chapter 8

Establishing and Maintaining Good Credit

If you've read this far, you already know about the importance of budgeting and the dangers of credit cards. But given our easy-credit society, you may see no reason to be nervous about taking on a little debt. Well, the thing about debt is that it's like hiking into the Grand Canyon—easy going in and rough climbing out. Lenders who seemed so friendly extending credit can become decidedly unfriendly later; and lenders are a talkative bunch—they never heard of "don't ask, don't tell". They will ask for their money back and tell their colleagues if they don't get it, ruining your chances of getting a loan later, when you might really need one. So, you should understand a "good credit rating" and how to maintain it.

Something that will probably strike you in this chapter is how many special laws we reference. These laws regulate granting credit, reporting credit, collecting on debts, etc. That laws were required should tip you off to the fact that these endeavors have been rife with abuse.

What is a credit record?

Basically, it's the history of the way you've handled money, a method of grading your financial health. Someone with a steady income, bills paid on time, and not too much debt has a good credit rating. These quali-fications and a track record of paying back loans on time produce an excellent credit rating. But, conversely, little income, multiple debts, and, worst of all, *failure to pay back a loan* ("default") ruin a rating.

How do I establish a credit record?

Whenever you pay (or don't pay) a bill or loan, you add a bit of data to your credit history. And the total of these bits becomes a financial pic-ture of you—your credit record—much of which is available through electronic data sharing among financial institutions. So, you establish a good credit record by engaging (responsibly) in financial transactions.

Getting a job is the first element in this record—the financial transac-tion is your receipt of a paycheck. Usually, the bigger the check, the more secure your rating, but steady income is also a factor. One check for writing a great movie script is not going to be as "credit worthy" as an equal amount received in salary, because a successful film might not be followed by another as successful, whereas paychecks will presum-ably continue. To establish your credit worthiness, a lender (also called a "creditor") takes into account all income you report on your credit application, including part time jobs, but can also take into account how long you have held those jobs and how likely they are to continue.

A savings, checking, or mutual fund account is also important. No bounced checks and some savings will show that you handle money prudently. After all, if you don't handle your money well, a lender has no reason to think you will be any more careful with *his/hers*. (Would you lend your favorite CD to someone who keeps his own discs scat-tered loose on the floor?)

Having a credit card will help you establish credit to get other cards. (Some are easier to get than others). You may need to start with a less favorable card and switch to a better card as your credit record evolves.

How does a lender use credit information?

Electronically-shared information (along, of course, with the application you fill out when you request any credit) will tell lenders what they need to know: (1) *Your ability to pay* (based upon income, usually salary) and expenses (including debts), *compared with the sum you want to borrow.* (2) *How financially* trustworthy you are. (Your other sterling traits, great looks, and cool clothes won't count for much here, unless they add to a sense of your ability to handle money responsibly and *repay on time*). However, some aspects of your *personal* life *will* count; staying at one address and in one job is generally favored over frequent migrations. (Of course, frequent moves to higher-paying jobs will be a plus). Finally, the type of loan and what **guarantees** you can provide for repayment are important. With a home mortgage loan, if you default, the lender can be reasonably sure that the house will be available to take back ("foreclose") and sell, to recoup the money lent to you. A car loan is less of a sure thing—the vehicle can be wrecked or driven to another state—but it provides at least some assurance. Other loans have fewer guarantees, so the bank may want to see "collateral" (items of financial value that can be available to the bank in case you default).

Are there any restrictions on what personal factors the lender can use to determine credit worthiness?

Yes. The Equal Credit Opportunity Act (ECOA) forbids discrimination on the basis of age, race, religion, marital status, gender, or national origin. Also, you can't be discriminated against because you are on public assistance or receiving government benefits of any sort, or because you disputed a charge—for example, you disputed what you believed to an error on your credit card statement (CHAPTER 7).

But, remember that while these factors *alone* cannot cause rejection of your credit application, they could indirectly count against you. Understandably, a banker might consider an individual whose income is limited to public assistance not creditworthy for a loan—because *the income itself* is insufficient or because the individual is not expected to continue to qualify for public assistance. Similarly, a lender might reasonably balk at making a loan, with a 30-year repayment schedule, to a 90-year-old. There is, of course, also a minimum age requirement—you have to be old enough to sign a legally-binding contract, usually age 18 or 21.

Gender and marital status present some interesting issues that may be important to you, especially if you are a woman. Traditionally, in this country, household expenses were billed to the husband and paid in his name. Therefore, the wife did not establish a separate credit record but was an appendage to her husband's account. If she then tried to establish her own credit worthiness, either because she wanted to take out a loan in her own name, or because she divorced, it was difficult. The ECOA corrected this unfairness by requiring that *both* partners in a marriage have their own credit records and that payments to an account be reported in *both* names. Incidentally, a woman can use her married name, her unmarried name, or both combined, but should stick to *one* of these and use it consistently, to have all of her credit history properly reported. (Conversely, when you are taking out a loan, the lender can ask for all names you use, or have used, so as to get all relevant records.)

Your marital status is relevant only to the extent that it affects your credit worthiness. So, you can't be turned down for credit *just because* you are single or married. *But*, a married person whose spouse has substantial debts may have difficulty getting a loan in "community property" states (Arizona, California, Idaho, Louisiana, Nevada, New Mexico, Texas, Washington, Wisconsin), and Puerto Rico, where husband and wife are legally liable for each other's debts! Therefore, the lender can require *your* application for a loan to include *your spouse's* credit record, and, in fact, may require your spouse's signature on the loan application. If you do *not* live in a community property state, and want to apply for credit based solely on *your* income, you cannot be compelled to include your spouse's signature on the application. However, if your spouse will have access to a credit card you receive, his/her credit record will also be included.

Alimony and child support payments will, of course, reveal the fact that you were married and/or that you have children; however, you have a choice about disclosing these payments—you can omit them, but then you can't have them included in an assessment of your eligibility for credit. And on the subject of children—a lender can ask how many dependent children you have, because they certainly represent a financial obligation. However, a lender *cannot* ask about your plans to have (more) children, or whether you use birth control.

What does a lender do with all of this information?

Each financial institution has its own system and standards for evaluating the data. Some use a scoring system that standardizes the process; others do not. So one legitimate lender may turn you down, while another equally legitimate lender approves your loan! But remember— *all legitimate lenders will be looking for the factors discussed above.* Be very careful if you are turned down by a number of legitimate lenders and then are offered terms that seem too good to be true by someone operating out of a newspaper ad, Internet posting, or storefront.

We discourage loans for recent graduates unless absolutely essential, and therefore we provide no further detailed information here. If you **must** take out a loan, try a credit union where you work before approaching a bank. If no credit union is available, terms are generally more favorable at savings banks or savings and loan associations than at commercial banks. No matter where the loan originates, be sure that you understand *all* terms and conditions before you sign. Remember: if you are turned down, *the lender must tell you why*, giving you the opportunity to correct any mistakes in your credit record and an understanding of what you must do to become creditworthy.

So why do I care about my credit record if I am not applying for a loan?

Usually, a loan is for a specific purpose, like a car or a house. If these are in your future, then you need to start building your credit record **now**.

Also, even if you are not applying for a loan, you may want a "line-of-credit" on your credit card or checking account. A line-of-credit is actually pre-approval for a loan. When applied to your checking account it is called "over-draft protection," a polite term for "bounced check protection." In other words, the bank lets you write checks—and pays them when they are presented—*even though your account is empty*. Obviously, the bank is lending you the money, and as you would surmise, the interest charged is steep. **Because this type of account is seductive in the extreme, we do not recommend it**, and even banks—which want you to go into debt and pay back interest year after year—assign a ceiling to your debt. (Will Struggleon simply cannot get $10,000 of "overdraft protection.") This arrangement differs from a regular loan in that the offer is there, ready for you to use, IF you want it, in the amounts you want, when you want, up to the ceiling set by the lender. For the established, responsible earner, this type of credit can be wonderful; it can protect against the occasional error when you write a check without sufficient funds in the bank (a bounce) or come in very handy for emergencies (stranded out-of-town in a blizzard). **But we strongly advise you to reject the offer of a line-of-credit for your checking account or credit card when you are starting out.**

How is my credit record tracked?

The grade you got in school was, for the most part, a matter between you and the professor. But in the world of lending, information is shared widely in a formal and structured manner, to catch proven deadbeats before anyone else lends them money, and discourage others from becoming deadbeats.

Credit bureaus, private companies with no connection to the Government, exist precisely for this purpose. Three *national* credit reporting systems (more information about them later) maintain records on an individual's financial health; many credit bureaus provide the information. A constant stream of data supplied by lenders and other companies with whom you have financial dealings flows into their computers. So, for example, if you have a credit card and pay all your bills on time, the credit bureaus will know, and the national systems will record this information. If you have loans and repay them according to the established schedule, credit bureaus think this is even better—it shows that you can be advanced money and stick to an agreement to pay it back.

If, however, you have defaulted on a loan, or if you have not defaulted but have a large amount of debt (mortgage, car loan, large credit card debt), they will know that too. In short, they know just about everything about you that your prospective mother-in-law would like to know. And although they may not tell your mother-in-law (unless she runs a bank), they will tell everyone else with a legitimate financial need to know. Notice that we said the report would have *most* of the information your prospective mother-in-law would like—the information is *only* financial in nature, although obviously it may disclose other related facts—your marital status, for example. But it does not—or should not—include information about morals, politics, or other personal matters.

Whenever you apply for any type of credit—car loan, mortgage, credit card—expect that your credit rating will be checked. Even some employers, particularly those whose employees may have access to company funds, will do a credit background check before hiring or promoting.

That sounds like a lot of information about me flowing back and forth. How do I know someone didn't make a mistake?

At first you don't—somebody might have. Fortunately, another law, the Fair Credit Reporting Act (FCRA), offers valuable protection. By the way, this law restricts access to your credit report to lenders, prospective employers, and others with a legitimate need to know. You, too, can now access your credit record to determine its accuracy. If you have been denied credit, you can get a **free** copy within 30 to 60 days. If you haven't been denied credit but would like to see your record anyway, a copy costs $8. The easiest way to get a copy is to contact one or more of the three national credit reporting systems—names and addresses appear at the end of this chapter. Incidentally, we have just started to hear ads from a company that for $29 will contact all three companies for you; although convenient, it is certainly no bargain.

If you find an error, contact the credit bureau that provided the information and ask that it be corrected. *The bureau is required to investigate any inaccuracy that you note, generally within 30 days.* If the bureau has provided incorrect information to a creditor within the past six months (or to a prospective employer within the past two years) you are entitled, by law, to have them send a corrected version. If you can't reach agreement, you have the right to have your side of the story included in the report (limit of 100 words). So, anyone who requests your credit record will also read your version of the circumstances behind any unpaid debt. To be sure that all future creditors will get the updated information, you will need to get credit reports from all three national systems. An automated process that will correct information in all three systems, when any one of them makes a correction, is under development.

Will a bad credit rating follow me forever?

Not necessarily, but it may seem that way. Generally, negative information has to be removed after seven years, but bankruptcies can remain on the record for as long as ten. The law also permits information obtained as part of an application for a job that pays more than $20,000/year to remain indefinitely; this also applies for information obtained as part of an application for more than $50,000 of credit or life insurance. Also, if financial information resulting from a lawsuit or judgment has a statute of limitations longer than seven years, that time limit applies. That's a long time to put on hold your plans for buying a home or worrying about what a future employer may find out. So avoiding a poor credit rating is extremely important.

What if I don't heed this advice and I get in trouble? What rights do I have? What rights does the creditor have?

Yet another law to your rescue: the Fair Debt Collection Practices Act (FCDPA). Sorry, this law doesn't protect you from having to pay debts. You still are responsible for all legitimate obligations. It does protect you from unfair collection practices by professional debt collectors acting on behalf of the creditor you owe. In other words, it does not cover the department store or bank you owe; it covers the "bill collector" that handles your overdue account.

You can, of course, get caught up in a situation where a debt collector has mistaken you for someone else or has incorrect information. Therefore, the first thing to know about your rights is that the collector must, within five days of first contact, tell you in writing how much you owe, whom you owe, and what to do if you disagree. Secondly, *you can ask the collector to verify the debt*; you must do this within 30 days of being contacted by the collector. The collector must then cease collection efforts until the debt has been verified and the collector has written to provide you with that verification. Note that this law does not cover your refusal to pay because you believe a product is faulty. In other words, you have no right under this law to continue withholding payment for that reason; the verification simply consists of ensuring that there is an actual debt, that the amount is as stated, and that you are the person who owes the money.

The law really concerns the tactics used by collectors. And in this area, you have significant rights. For example, collectors cannot use abusive or threatening language; they cannot pretend to be government agents or give you incorrect legal information. They can't call at obviously inconvenient times (though of course, if you're still observing your sleeping schedule from college, you probably prefer a call at 2 a.m. to one at 2 p.m.). And perhaps most important, **they cannot tell your employer or a neighbor or any other third party without authorization from either you or the courts.** Note, though, a fine distinction under this law: the collector can contact a third party, like your employer, to get your address, if you are not represented by an attorney, but the collector *cannot* tell the third party why he is seeking the information. Also, the collector can, and probably will, report the status of the debt collection to credit bureaus; they are not prohibited third parties.

And how do I re-establish a good credit record?

The bottom-line advice from consumer credit professionals is twofold: 1) it takes some time, personal effort, and serious planning to get out of trouble and 2) you can do it yourself and probably should not pay money for a credit repair clinic or other business that promises to fix your credit problems for you. These companies often promise miracles; they sometimes claim they can wipe out bad credit records and restore your credit. They cannot deliver and will only drive you further into debt by charging for the non-delivered services. In fact, abuses in this area led to a regulation prohibiting telemarketing credit repair companies from requiring customers to pay until six months after their services have been delivered. That should tell you something.

What you should do is what you should have been doing all along—manage your money and live within your income. There are no miracles other than winning the lottery (we don't suggest you count on this cure—you have a better chance of guessing some stranger's entire ten-digit phone number). Seek professional credit counselors —not quick fix artists—who will counsel you on how to live within a budget and help you work with creditors to construct a repayment plan.

Most creditors are willing to work with professional credit counselors, because getting at least *some* money without further collection efforts is cost-beneficial to them. Usually these counseling services are reached through non-profit organizations; they will charge nothing (or only a minimal fee). An especially helpful source is the Consumer Credit Counseling Service, with offices in almost every state. Call the National Foundation for Consumer Credit (301-589-5600) for a referral near you. Follow their advice; **it does work**. If someone wants a large fee, or promises immediate solutions, stay clear or you will never set your record straight.

If you've read this chapter carefully and know your rights and obligations, you can take credit for not becoming a credit victim.

Appendix

NATIONWIDE CREDIT REPORTING SYSTEMS

Experian
National Consumer Assistance Center
P.O.Box 949
Allen, Texas 75013
800 682 7654

Equifax Credit Information Services, Inc.
P.O. Box 740241
Atlanta, Georgia 30374-0241
800 685 1111

Trans Union Corporation
Trans Union Consumer Relations
760 West Sproul Road, P.O. Box 390
Springfield, Pennsylvania 19064-0390
800 645 1533

Chapter 9

Repaying Student Loans

If you have no student loans, skip this chapter, but if you have one, read on, to understand your obligations and rights. (This chapter does NOT cover how to get a loan; we assume you are past that, so we will deal only with repayment issues. If you or your family needs information about applying for a student loan, call 1-800-4-FED-AID or visit the web site at www.edgov/offices/OPE/agencies.html. (Ability to remember that address will probably qualify you immediately for a loan, if not a scholarship).

But even if you do have a student loan, you need not grind through this entire chapter. Start by reading **THE BASICS** section and then **skip to the specific type of loan you have.** BUT, you must also check the loan documents originally issued by your lender and/or school. One of these is a promissory note, a legally-binding agreement to repay the debt. This note, which you signed, stipulates the conditions under which the loan is, and is not, due. If that document appears to contradict information here or elsewhere, do not assume you misunderstand the promissory note. For clarification, check with your school or lender, or with the U. S. Department of Education, to be sure you understand the terms and conditions that apply.

FEDERAL PELL GRANTS are not covered here, because they are not loans and require no repayment. Similarly, FEDERAL SUPPLEMENTAL EDUCATIONAL OPPORTUNITY GRANTS are not repaid. If these are what you had in school, skip to CHAPTER 10.

PLUS Loans are for parents, so we omit them too. Many PLUS loan provisions (for example, on cancellation of the debt) are similar to those of the student loans discussed below, but your parents should contact the lender or the loan servicing center for needed clarification.

BASICS:

Student loans have several advantages over standard loans (home mortgages and car loans). First, you generally do not have to establish strict credit worthiness (CHAPTER 8) to get one: the lending institution recognizes that when you take out the loan you probably don't have the ability to immediately begin repaying (and it can't take your diploma as collateral if you default!). Second, your repayment is long-delayed—not canceled, but deferred; for a car loan this would be like buying a car and driving it for years before payments begin. Third, and this is a critical point, when the loan is based on financial need, *you will not start owing interest* when the loan is awarded; that is, interest is *not charged* until you graduate. We do not simply mean that interest payments are deferred; we actually mean that no interest is ever charged to your account for the years of your education! Such a loan, which saves you a bundle, is called "subsidized" and is extremely desirable. However, some student loans not based upon financial need, are unsubsidized, and accumulate interest owed from their inception.

By the way, "elimination" of interest charges is not a gift from your local banker. Banks issue loans to make money. The federal government makes these loans possible *by paying the interest to your bank for you while you are in school.* (You should feel a little better about taxes knowing that part of your tax dollar is going to help future students in the same way older taxpayers helped you.) The Free Scholarship Search Service on the Internet calculated that if you received the maximum subsidized loan each year for four years, and began repayment six months after graduation, the interest payments you avoided (i.e., what the Government paid on your behalf) could be $5200! Student loans are a big business.

If you have an *unsubsidized* loan and made no interest payments in college, you now must repay the original amount of money borrowed (the "principal") and, at long last, the interest that was owed when you were in school, as well as the interest that continues to accumulate after graduation. This process is called "capitalization." Perhaps the term "capitalization" is appropriate, because, as we'll see later, the process can land you in Trouble, with a capital "T"; interest that accumulated while you were in school adds to interest accumulating after graduation, and when payback of principal is included, you face a mountain of debt.

As intuition suggests, the longer you take to repay a loan, the smaller each payment will be. HOWEVER, interest is charged for the life of the loan, and, **therefore, the longer you take to repay the loan, the more you will pay in total.** Confused? If you borrow $20,000.00 and pay it off slowly, principal and interest, over thirty years, each payment would be smaller than if you paid it off over 15 years, but **the sum** of all payments (principal and interest) over the 30-year schedule will be MUCH greater than the sum of all payments over 15 years—not just twice as great, **but much more.** This happens because you pay interest for a longer time, in return for the privilege of stretching out the loan. Therefore, all things being equal, **you should pay off any loan, including a student loan,** *as quickly as possible.* However, occasionally other factors intervene; for example, if you are paying very low loan interest, say 5%, and you can earn somewhat more than 5% by investing in a mutual fund, you may consider it worthwhile to repay less each month and invest (**NOT SPEND**) the remainder; **this would be especially true for an IRA, where a tax deduction and tax-deferred earnings are on your side.** But—do not be fooled into thinking that low payments for a long time are actually saving you money; you will be paying much more interest on the loan and hoping to more than make up for that increase with successful investments and the tax advantages of an IRA.

Mercifully, the tax laws of 1997 permit some hefty tax deductions for interest on student loans (CHAPTER 5).

STAFFORD DIRECT AND FFEL LOANS:

Your student loan is probably one of these. The full name of the Direct Loan is "William D. Ford Federal Direct Loan Program"; FFEL stands for "Federal Family Education Loan Program". Direct loans come directly (hence the name) from the Federal Government; FFEL loans come through an institution, like a bank. Although similar, there are some repayment differences, so be sure you know which type you have before reading on.

Note that Direct or FFEL Stafford loans first awarded after July 1, 1994 can *never* charge more than 8.25% interest. The rate will be adjusted each July 1 for the life of the loan.

DIRECT LOAN REPAYMENT OPTIONS:

These loans feature four repayment options. When you have completed school, select one. However, a review is worthwhile, because, as we will see later, you may switch (consolidate) your loan and change the repayment plan you have already chosen. The plans are:

(1)Standard Repayment

Under this Plan, you pay a fixed amount each month until your loan is fully paid back. The monthly amount must be at least $50, and you must pay an amount each month that will completely repay the loan within 10 years. The maximum interest rate is 8.25%. Using this rate, the Department of Education gives the following example: If you owe $10,000 and pay $123 each month, you will actually have paid a total of $14,718 by the time the loan is paid off. ($4718.00 of that total is interest.)

(2)Extended Repayment

Under this option, you can take 12 to 30 years to repay your loan. The minimum payment is $50. With such a long repayment schedule, the payment may be fairly low each month, but stretching the payments over such a long time also means that you will eventually pay a **MUCH** higher **total** amount, because you will be paying interest on the unpaid balance for many extra years. Using the Department of Education computation for repaying $10,000 under this option, and using a monthly payment of $97, you would ultimately pay back **$17,463! Remember this when you later buy a house; a fifteen-year mortgage loan beats a thirty-year loan hands down** (assuming that you can handle the larger monthly payments of the shorter payment schedule).

(3)Graduated Repayment

This plan can be attractive to many students, because it recognizes the basic fact that your earnings should increase over the years. Your payments are not fixed at a pre-set amount each month for the life of the repayment schedule (as they are for

Standard and Extended payments). Rather, you pay smaller monthly amounts at the beginning and then the amount increases—generally, every two years. You can take 12 to 30 years to repay (depending on the size of the loan). But again, remember the basic concept—a longer repayment schedule means greater total payment.

Using that same Department of Education example, the $10,000 loan may have monthly repayments as low as $70, but **the total paid will be $19,085!!** That is virtually twice as much as you initially borrowed.

(4)Income Contingent Repayment

This option is an interesting variation. It recognizes that some individuals will flourish and can pay off their loans quickly; others, *for any number of reasons*, will not fare so well and will never be able to pay off the loan. Therefore, repayments are keyed to yearly income, family size, and loan amount. Your payments vary with income, and after 25 years any unpaid balance is eliminated.

In some ways, this plan is closer to insurance than a standard loan—it recognizes that some people will draw heavily on the benefit (not repay a significant portion of the loan) and some will never need the benefit (they will repay more than their fair share). Using our two examples of I. Will Struggleon and Dr. Richard Thanyou, and assuming both received college loans and elected this repayment option, it is possible that if Will's income never significantly rises, only a fraction of his loan will ever be repaid; however, Dr. Thanyou will pay back the entire loan with interest.

Again, using the Department of Education example, and assuming a yearly income of $25,000, an unmarried individual might make a monthly payment of $92 and eventually pay $17,850.

FFEL REPAYMENT OPTIONS:

FFEL loans feature three repayment options, similar to options 1, 3 and 4 above, but the specifics within each category may vary from lender to lender more than for Direct loans. The options are:

(1)Standard

A fixed sum is paid each month, with a minimum of $50 of the interest that has accrued. Using the Department of Education example, a $10,000 loan with a monthly payment of $123 results in a total payment of $14,718.

(2)Graduated Repayment

Your monthly payment increases over time, but never more than by a factor of three—i.e., no monthly payment can be greater than three times the lowest monthly payment. The $10,000 loan with a monthly payment of $69 would result in a total payment of $16,012.

(3)Income-Sensitive Repayment

Like the income contingent Direct option, your payments vary. Income sensitive monthly payments are based upon your yearly income and the loan amount. No planned monthly payment may be more than three times higher than the lowest monthly payment, and each payment must at a minimum pay off interest accrued since the last payment. An unmarried individual with an income of $25,000, paying back $10,000 under this plan, may have a payment in some months of $83, and the total repayment will be $17,783.

This type of loan you are expected to continue paying until it is paid in full, unlike the Direct Income Contingent loan.

When you start payment on Direct and FFEL Stafford loans:

The great thing about Stafford loans is that you do not begin repayment immediately. In fact, while you are in school at least half time, you make no loan payments (unless you are receiving an *unsubsidized* Stafford loan, in which case you may pay on the interest only). This approach lets you concentrate on your education. Understandably, therefore, your repayments begin when any one of the following applies:

- you graduate

- you drop out of school (Failure to graduate is NOT a legitimate reason to stop paying.)

- your enrollment drops below half-time.

The Department of Education's definition of "half-time" is: "At schools measuring progress by credit hours and semesters, trimesters, or quarters, half time enrollment is at least six semester hours or quarter hours per term. At schools measuring progress by credit hours but not using semesters, trimesters, or quarters, half-time enrollment is at least 12 semester hours or 18 quarter hours per year. At schools measuring progress by clock hours, half time enrollment is at least 12 hours per week. Note that schools may choose to set higher minimums than these."

In all of these cases, the government recognizes that you need a period of adjustment—hopefully, that period will include finding a job that makes repayment possible. Therefore, when any of the above three circumstances arise, you have a "grace period" of six months before repayment starts. For subsidized loans, no interest is charged during this grace period.

PAYMENT DEFERMENT, FORBEARANCE, AND CANCELLATION OF STAFFORD LOANS:

Loans are serious business, and the government, your school, and your lender expect repayment on time. But life is choppy, and there can be compelling and acceptable reasons why you may need an exemption from the agreed-upon payment plan. If your reasons are valid, you may qualify for **deferment, forbearance, or cancellation.**

Even if you appear to qualify, deferments, forbearances and cancellations are not automatic. You must contact your Direct Loan servicing center or your lender; documentation may be required. You should continue to make payments, if at all possible, until you are formally notified that your request is approved.

DEFERMENT:

A deferment is a temporary postponement of payments. During this period of deferment, interest doesn't continue to accrue. For loans disbursed after July 1, 1993, these circumstances can justify deferment:

● enrollment at least half time at a post-secondary school

● studying in an approved graduate fellowship program or in an approved rehabilitation training program for the disabled

●inability to find full-time employment (this deferment may last up to 3 years)

Note that service in VISTA or in the Peace Corps does not automatically qualify for a deferment. However, an individual serving in such programs may qualify on economic grounds for a deferment.

FORBEARANCE:

A "forbearance" may sometimes be granted to individuals who do not meet deferment requirements. Forbearances are granted for a limited and specific interval and may involve either a postponement of payments or a reduction in monthly payments, but interest continues to accrue. (Ultimately, however, the loan must be repaid). The criteria are less strict than for deferral and typically include:

●service in a medical or dental internship or residency

●service in a position under the National Community Service Trust Act of 1993

●payments on certain federal student loans equal to or greater than 20% of monthly gross income

CANCELLATION:

Understandably, cancellations are extremely difficult to obtain, and for the most part, you would not want to meet the criteria:

●borrower's death

●borrower's total and permanent disability

●bankruptcy: To qualify for this provision, seven years must have passed between the date payments were to begin and the date that the borrower files for bankruptcy. Periods of deferment or forbearance do not count towards this seven-year period. If seven years have not passed, a bankruptcy court must rule that repayment would cause undue hardship.

●school closed (for loans received on or after 1/1/86) before the student could complete a program of study, or school falsely certified the loan.

For unsubsidized loans, interest is charged during grace periods, deferments, and forbearance.

FEDERAL PERKINS LOANS:

Perkins loans apply to students with exceptional financial need and guarantee an interest rate of only 5%. These loans use Federal Government funds; but since they are administered through schools, the repayment is to the school, so you must contact that school if you have any repayment questions.

Like Stafford loans, payments vary with the size of the loan and the duration of repayment; deferment, forbearance, or cancellation are also possible under certain circumstances. Again, the process is not automatic. You must apply (in this case, to the school) and receive approval before you can stop payments.

DEFERMENT:

Deferments postpone (but do not cancel) payment obligations. During the deferment period no interest charges accrue. You may apply to your school for a deferment under the following circumstances:

- studying at least half time at a post-secondary school (see the definition of half time under Stafford loan deferments)

- studying in an approved graduate fellowship program or an approved rehabilitation program for the disabled

- inability to find full-time employment (deferment may be granted for up to 3 years)

- economic hardship (up to 3 years)

- working in certain types of service, which can include:

  - full-time teacher in a designated elementary or secondary school serving students from low income families

  - full-time special education teacher in a non-profit elementary or secondary school (for loans on or after 7/1/93)

  - full-time qualified professional provider of early intervention services for the disabled (for loans on or after 7/1/93)

  - full-time teacher of math, science, foreign languages, bilingual education, or other fields designated as "teacher shortage" areas (for loans on or after 7/1/93)

  - full-time employee of a public or non-profit child or family service agency providing services to high risk children and their families from low income communities (for loans on or after 7/1/93)

❖full-time nurse or medical technician (for loans on or after 7/1/93)

❖service as a full-time law enforcement or corrections officer (for loans on or after 7/1/93)

❖full-time service as a staff member in the educational component of a Head Start program

❖service as a VISTA or Peace Corps volunteer

❖service in the armed forces in areas of hostilities or imminent danger

FORBEARANCE:

An approved forbearance allows you to temporarily stop making payments; however, interest continues to accrue. Forbearances can be approved for up to 12 consecutive months, for up to three years and can be granted if you are unable to meet your payment schedule but do not qualify for a deferment. Typically, such circumstances would be serious (but not permanent) health problems, temporary economic difficulties, or financial obligations.

CANCELLATION:

For Perkins loans, many situations qualify; some are not options you would want, **but many relate to your occupation and could be attractive.**

- borrower's death

- borrower's total and permanent disability

- full-time teacher in a designated elementary or secondary school serving students from low income families

- full-time special education teacher in a non-profit elementary or secondary school

- full-time qualified professional provider of early intervention services for the disabled (for loans on or after 7/23/92)

- full-time teacher of math, science, foreign languages, bilingual education, or other fields designated as "teacher shortage areas" (for loans on or after 7/23/92)

- full-time employee of a public or non-profit child or family service agency providing services to high-risk children and their families from low income communities (for loans on or after 7/23/92)

- full-time nurse or medical technician (for loans on or after 7/23/92)

- service as a full-time law enforcement or corrections officer (for loans on or after 11/29/90)

- full-time service as a staff member in the educational component of a Head Start program

- service as a VISTA or Peace Corps volunteer (up to 70% of the loan may be canceled)

- service in the armed forces (up to 50% canceled) in areas of hostilities or imminent danger. Note that the armed services may also pay, on your behalf, a portion of your Perkins loan, as an enlistment incentive)

●bankruptcy. Periods of deferment or forbearance do not count towards this seven-year period. If seven years have not passed, a bankruptcy court must rule that repayment would cause undue hardship.

CONSOLIDATION LOANS:

To pay for your education, you may have taken out more than one loan; perhaps you have a Stafford subsidized Direct loan and also an unsubsidized FFEL loan. Or perhaps you have chosen a repayment plan that you are unhappy with. Or perhaps the interest rate you are paying is higher than a rate you could get now. For any of these reasons, or for others, you may feel that you would like to get one new loan for repayment purposes; this new loan is not to provide new spending money but to consolidate the loans you already have (or provide a new repayment plan, if you have just one loan) so as to create better repayment terms. **Any of the loans discussed in this chapter can potentially qualify for consolidation, and you have two consolidation loan options for the new loan: Direct and FFEL.**

Consolidation loans may be an excellent tool, if your current loans are burdensome or not giving you the best available rates. But before consolidating loans be sure you fully understand this very technical process. For more information about loan consolidations in general, or to find out how consolidation would work for you specifically, call **The Department of Education Loan Origination Center's Consolidation Department at 1-800 557-7392 (hearing impaired, 1-800-557-7395).**

DIRECT AND FFEL CONSOLIDATION LOANS:

When: Virtually anytime during the payment process—during your grace period, once you have started payments, or during deferment or forbearance.

What: You may consolidate any or all student loans, but at least one must already be a Direct or FFEL loan. However, if you do not have a Direct loan, but do have a FFEL loan, you are required to first contact a provider of FFEL Consolidation loans. (There are then special provisions that determine whether you can receive a consolidation loan). For answers to such questions, call the toll free number listed above. Also, if you are still in school, or if you have defaulted on a student loan, special eligibility requirements apply.

(Incidentally, consolidation is also possible for Direct PLUS loans—the ones your parents have to deal with).

PAYMENT PLANS FOR DIRECT CONSOLIDATION LOANS:

Payment options are the same as those for Direct loans (standard, extended, graduated, and income contingent), except that Direct PLUS loans do not qualify for Income Contingent repayment plans. Interest rates for Direct subsidized and unsubsidized consolidation loans cannot exceed 8.25%; Direct PLUS consolidation loans cannot exceed 9%. The rates are set each July 1.

How: Direct consolidation loans are administered by the U.S. Government. To apply, call the toll free number.

PAYMENT PLANS FOR FFEL CONSOLIDATION LOANS:

When: During the grace period or once your repayment begins.

What: All repayment options (standard, graduated and income sensitive) are available. However, there are many restrictions in the FFEL consolidation process:

- Direct loans cannot be consolidated into a FFEL loan

- If all loans being consolidated are subsidized, you'll receive a subsidized loan. If ANY loan you receive is not subsidized, ALL loans being consolidated will become unsubsidized. This is very important, because you will be losing the more favorable terms of your subsidized loans. For example, with subsidized loans, you do not have to worry about interest accruing during deferments.

- The interest rate for the consolidation loan will be the weighted average of the original interest rates of the loans being consolidated, rounded up to the nearest whole percent. This means that the percentage is automatically calculated, and you cannot shop around for a better rate, as you can with car loans, for example.

Before you consider consolidation, be sure you understand all the terms and conditions: what happens if your income increases, if you need a deferment, etc.? For example, you may imagine that getting a lower rate of interest is going to make a real difference in your payments. But take a look at an actual example, as calculated by the Free Scholarship web site: Someone paying off a $10,000 loan in 120 payments at 9.00% interest, will have a monthly payment of $122.65. If that individual succeeds in getting a loan at only 7.43% interest, the monthly payment is $111.02. The net savings is about $10 per month, or $120 per year. That's certainly better, but not dramatically so; a small change in your interest rate may produce only a very small gain.

If you are not sure or are uncomfortable with these kinds of mechanics, bring along someone who understands them. Don't be embarrassed to involve your parents in the conversation—parents are out to protect your interests; bankers are out to protect their "interest" (preferably compounded daily and growing as fast as possible!).

LOAN PREPAYMENT

Generally, student loans permit you to *prepay* ahead of schedule. If you are paying a high interest rate on your loan, you may find that you are better off paying larger amounts than your plan calls for each month. As we have seen, the longer you take to pay off a loan, the more money you eventually pay. Early payment, if your financial picture permits, can be wise. It helps establish an excellent credit record and will help when you apply for other loans, like a mortgage.

IMPACT OF STUDENT LOAN REPAYMENTS ON YOUR CREDIT RATING

Defaults are serious. Although the rules are stringent, individuals with legitimate problems (like health) can find legitimate alternatives to default. Nevertheless, many people simply walk away from their obligations, with out any good faith effort to comply. We believe that repayment obligations should be honored, but, morality aside, practical factors should drive you to honor your financial commitments. And those practical reasons relate to credit worthiness (chapter 8).

Surprisingly, even if you do not receive a billing notice, your obligation to pay on schedule remains. So, if your lender slips up one month, and you don't receive a notice, keep up with your payments anyway. If you wait, when the lender catches up you will probably owe interest on the late payments. And, by the way, you are legally obliged to inform your lender of any relevant facts like a change in address or name. One twist on this is that *your lender's name* may change. Commonly, lenders sell their loans (they are an asset to the lender, since they are profitable) to another financial institution. You have no control over this process but be sure to send payment to the correct company. So, if you are sending a payment, don't look at some old billing information for the address—use the current bill. If you send a payment to the previous lender, you may have difficulty getting your money back and will owe late fees to the current lender.

If you fail to pay in accordance with the promissory note you originally signed (as modified, of course, by any later officially authorized changes, like deferments or consolidations), problems will follow:

(1) The lender (a bank, your school, or a government agency) will try to collect the money owed. You will be held responsible for collection costs, possible court costs, etc. The national credit bureaus will be notified. This kind of track record may well ruin your chance of getting a loan in the future and will prevent you from getting a government loan if you return to school in the future.

(2) The Government may also try to collect its money through the Internal Revenue Service or any other Government agency that owes you money. For example, if you are owed a tax refund, **the IRS may withhold that refund and apply it towards your unpaid loan.** If you were counting on that refund for your IRA investment, you're out of luck.

(3) The lender may go to court for an order that deducts payments from your company paycheck. This, at a minimum, would be embarrassing, but it could also hurt your career. For example, if your job involves access to company funds, or if your integrity is vital to the boss's opinion, the company may have second thoughts about promoting you.

(4) Finally, default CAN have a severe negative impact if you are in a field that requires a professional license (e.g., a doctor or lawyer). The government may notify the state licensing board, which can, in turn, revoke your professional license! And truly, this seems appropriate, because your license was obtained through education money from the government in the first place.

THE BOTTOM LINE:

If you have trouble paying back a student loan, seek relief appropriate to your particular loan type, but DON'T DEFAULT. REMEMBER: from a credit rater's perspective, *DEFAULT IS YOUR FAULT.*

Chapter 10

Putting it All Together

Before setting our plan in motion, you will have to open a checking account, decide upon the saving method that works for you, and find out if you can get a little financial help.

(1) The checking account:

Open a checking account with the lowest possible ATM fees, the lowest fees for each check, the lowest monthly balance, and the lowest monthly maintenance fees. Ignore interest paid on your balance.

Many student accounts apply, so set one up before you graduate, if possible, and keep mum about your graduation. (A credit union, if available, is also a good option for some banking functions).

Try to withdraw cash from an ATM only once each week, and if your account limits you to only a few checks per month, use a debit card to pay for everything you can, saving your checks for the few bills that require them—like rent. *Stay out of debit card debt by deducting each debit card transaction from your checkbook register each evening. FOLLOW SECURITY PRECAUTIONS FOR ATM/DEBIT CARDS, AS EXPLAINED IN CHAPTER 4.*

If possible, use "on line" or "PC" banking to pay bills electronically; payments are automatically deducted from your checking account balance as part of the program, and you avoid fees for writing too many checks.

Checking account established, you are now ready to consider the savings plan that works for you.

(2) Think about your savings plan:

Are you a self-disciplined saver, who can put aside a set sum from each check—"paying yourself first", before spending ANYTHING? If so, you are home free, but if this is like asking a hungry tiger to delicately refuse raw meat, you have two good alternatives:

Best option: ask your payroll department to sign you up for an automatic payroll savings plan, which deducts a pre-set sum from each paycheck for automatic deposit in the account of your choice—bank or credit union. (Before signing up try to make a realistic estimate of how much less money you can live on per week—that is, how much you can save. This "guesstimate" will give you an idea of how much you will have saved by the end of the year.) If your payroll department responds to your request like a dog to cat food, move on to "plan B".

Plan B: then you use the automatic withholding mechanism to save and deposit your tax refund into your IRA. We can almost guarantee that you, the unmotivated saver, really will deposit your tax refund into an IRA, because you will have entered information on your tax return that *requires the IRA deposit* (upon penalty of tax law violation), and we think you *will enter this information on your tax return*, because the entry WILL LOWER YOUR FEDERAL TAXES—who can resist that? Sound interesting? Read on...

(Incidentally, "plan B" is universally considered worse than saving on your own, because while the government has your money it is not invested for you. But "plan b" is better than no plan at all. So, if your payroll office won't go for automatic deposits from your check, and you spend everything you pocket and in your bank account, "plan b" is your ticket.)

(3) Are you totally on your own?:

Can you get a financial "jump start" from parent(s), grandparent(s), or any significant other? We emphasize that a lot of parents will be much more receptive to helping you start an IRA than to doling out cash for living expenses. They know (or, if they don't, try telling them, or better yet, ask them to read chapter three of this book) that under current law you can't access the money until age 59 1/2, (except for a very few "responsible" causes), that it will accumulate tax-deferred for years and years, that you can probably take a large tax deduction (depending on your income), and that an IRA is the ultimate badge of responsibility. Stress that an IRA will get you into the investing game and stimulate you to follow the markets, **and their initial hefty donation to your IRA can be a one-time event, because after you have met the minimum deposit required to start an S&P 500 Index Fund account, you can make much smaller subsequent contributions on your own.**

At last, checking account established, savings style determined, and help given (or denied) for your IRA, it's time to get started:

If you can get financial help: ESTABLISH YOUR IRA IMMEDIATELY. The longer it is in place, the longer it will work for you.

Call one of the mutual fund companies that has an S&P 500 Index Fund (Chapter 2) or call Fidelity Mutual Funds (Chapter 3). **Fidelity's Spartan Market Index Fund (800-544-6666) has a minimum IRA investment of only $500. Alternatively, use the TIAA-CREF Growth and Income Fund, a no-load fund with a minimum deposit of only $250.**

Remember: To take a tax deduction for a given calendar year (for example, January 1, 2000 to December 30, 2000) you must make your IRA contribution by April 15 of the next calendar year, in this case April 15, 2001. Does this mean that an IRA started after April 15, 2001 is worthless as a tax deduction? NO!! You would use any contributions made after April 15, 2001 for tax year 2001, and you would have until April 15, 2002 to reach your maximum contribution.

If you are on your own, and—

YOU ARE A SELF-MOTIVATED SAVER:

(a)   Open a bank savings account and salt away as much as you can afford from each paycheck until you reach $500, the minimum required by **Fidelity's Spartan Market Index Fund.** If you can actually save $3000 on your own, so much the better—go with Vanguard.

(b)   Alternative method: Begin an IRA with the **TIAA CREF Growth and Income** Fund, as explained above.

YOU ARE A POORLY-MOTIVATED SAVER, but if the money disappears from your paycheck *before you ever see it*, you'll be cool:

Sign up for an *automatic payroll savings plan*; money will be deducted from your paycheck and deposited in the bank or credit union of your choice before you see it. (Payroll departments usually won't do this with mutual fund companies directly). Start an IRA when you have saved enough in your bank or credit union.

The problem with this plan is that you may be unable to resist spending the money accumulating in the bank; it may never get to an IRA. So, ask your bank if automatic payroll savings deductions from your paycheck can go *directly into a bank IRA.* The great virtue of a bank IRA is that it can often be started with as little as $25 or $50!!

Even if the bank IRA pays a low interest rate, even if it isn't an S&P 500 Index Fund, any IRA is better than no IRA! Remember: You can easily switch money from your initial IRA into a better investment later: *getting started is key.*

YOU ARE A POORLY-MOTIVATED SAVER AND A DEDICATED CONSUMER/SPENDER, so an automatic payroll deduction plan that puts money directly into your bank savings account or credit union isn't for you, because when savings build up, it's party time, OR your payroll department won't (or can't) deposit money directly into a bank IRA:

Use the automatic withholding mechanism in combination with tax law. Step by step, here's how the system works:

(1) Go to your payroll department, and change the number of exemptions on your W4 to FEWER than you really have. For example, if you are a single, unmarried worker, you have probably written ONE exemption (meaning one dependent—yourself) on your W4; change this to ZERO. After a "lag period" for the paperwork to go through, federal and state tax withheld from each of your paychecks will automatically increase, and your take-home pay will drop, so you will have a little less to live on. (Ask your payroll department to first calculate how much this

maneuver will reduce your take-home pay, so you won't be in for any nasty surprises. If your pay drops too far, don't panic; **you are entitled to change the number of exemptions on your W4 as often as you wish.**)

(2) Make a reasonable estimate of how much of a refund you will receive. If you are just starting out, single, with no dependents, no mortgage, and no significant major other deductions (like extensive charitable contributions, medical expenses, etc.), the change from **ONE** dependent to **ZERO** dependents should result in a refund of several hundred dollars; even a worker at Will Struggleon's meager income level should realize a refund of over $300.00. If you want a more precise estimate, run your tax data through one of the software programs discussed in CHAPTER 5, using identical entries for all data but using **ONE** exemption for the first calculation and **ZERO** exemptions for the second.

(3) Believe it or not, the standard W-4 allows you to indicate whether you would like *additional* money withheld from your paycheck above and beyond the withholding calculated on the basis of your income and number of exemptions. In other words, if all of your withholds were to total $54 per check, and you decide to "save" $5 more from each check, you can indicate that $59 is to be withheld. **So, consider requesting $5 to $10 additional withholding from each paycheck; you won't miss such a small sum, but your annual refund will increase by $150 to $250.**

(4) When you fill out your 1040 or 1040-EZ, list an IRA contribution the size of your *projected* refund or a little larger. THIS WILL FUR-THER LOWER YOUR TAX BILL AND INCREASE YOUR REFUND IN MOST CASES (CHAPTER 3), *but it commits you to making the IRA contribution.*

(5) **File your tax return early, preferably by the third week of February, so your refund will arrive well before April 15.** You will need your

refund early so you will have time to make your IRA deposit before the April 15 deadline.

(6) When your refund arrives, set up your IRA **at once.** You'll be tempted to spend the refund, but **you know that you are now committed to the IRA, based upon the tax form you filed!** (By the way, you can request that the IRS send your refund **directly** to a bank or some other financial institution.)

Now, after starting your IRA, move on to saving for short- and medium-range goals. Use the methods outlined above, depositing money in non-IRA accounts. Because most non-IRA mutual funds (with a few notable exceptions like the TIAA-CREF Growth and Income Fund) initially require at least $1000, you may have to start by directing automatic payroll deductions to a bank "money market account" or using the automatic withholding mechanism to architect a large refund.

Because stock market downturns are inevitable, and because you are saving for the short- and medium-term as well as for retirement, **about half of your non-IRA money should stay in "safe" accounts**, like a lowly bank savings account, a bank "money market account," or, better yet, a simple "money market mutual fund," all of which insulate you from market fluctuations.

Congratulations! You are on your way!

About the Authors

Zachary D. Grossman, Professor at the State University of New York at Buffalo, is a prize-winning teacher and lecturer. His wife, Justine, co-owns and manages a small business. His daughter is a 1998 college graduate, his stepson is a college freshman, and his son is a stockbroker.

Janis Gade Landis is a Regional Comptroller of the United States Treasury Department. Her husband is Professor and Chair of the Political Science Department of Hofstra University. Their elder daughter is a college senior, and their younger daughter is a college freshman.

Appendix

Day Trading: Nightmare or Dream-Come-True

Well, why not? Everybody's doing it, right? Twelve-year-olds glued to their computers making more on AOL shares in two-and-one-half hours than your father did in 3 years, any stock offering that ends in ".com" multiplying in value by a factor of 20 or 30 in a single day, and a blizzard of ads that tout the chic, hype, and confidence of the smug on-line investing crowd. So, join the party!

What actually is "Day Trading"?

"Day Trading" is buying and selling a single stock within one trading day. In other words, you buy the stock, monitor it all day, and sell when you can make a profit.

By the way, "day-trading" is often confused with "on-line trading." Virtually all "day-trading" is performed on-line, because the commissions for buying and selling stock on-line are low enough to make real profits possible from very small rises in a stock's price, but most on-line buying and selling is by investors with no interest in price variations that occur during a single day; these on-line investors buy though the Net because it is cheaper, and very often, more convenient.

Did you say monitor it all day?

Yup. Because a stock may begin its day ("open") at a certain price, fall in price, rise again, fall again, and gyrate throughout the day, closing at the end of the day at a higher, lower, or the same price that it opened at. So, in order to sell ("liquidate your position" or "get out") while you have a profit, **you must remain in constant touch.**

Wait a minute. Does this mean that I could miss a lot of opportunities if I trade between classes?

You bet.

O.K., O.K., I get it. I take the money I earned over the summer and spend two weeks in August sitting at my computer, full-time, playing this game. Where do I start?

First, start by deciding how much money you can afford to lose.

You're kidding. Where did you get all this negativity?

From experience.

Whose experience?

Everybody's! Studies of day-traders show that *at least 75%* of them lose more money than they earn. And, because people hate to admit losses in the market, this percentage may be distorted; in other works, *more than 75% probably lose.*

So we just throw up our hands and walk away?

Not at all, but as we said, you first decide how much money you can afford to lose.

Five thousand dollars.

Too much. Unless your name is Bill Gates, try again.

Two thousand dollars.

Close, but no cigar, unless you are already rich.

One thousand.

O.K. Now to find out if you really think you can tolerate a loss on $1000, apply the casino test.

The What?

The casino test. Ask this question: "Would I be perfectly comfortable taking this money to Las Vegas for casino gambling?"

If the answer is "yes," proceed. If the answer is "no," put your $1000 in the TIAA-CREF Growth and Income Fund. Or, if you must buy a stock on line, for peer approval and conversation at the cigar bar or health club, buy Dow Diamonds or SPIDERS.

I'm ready. What's next.

Start an on-line brokerage account. Most every firm can quote a survey that rates it number one. Your limiting factor, however, is the minimum investment that the firm will handle. In a few hours of cNBC you'll see ads for 5 or 6 on-line firms, and ads in the Wall Street Journal can provide several more. Open an account with the firm that will accept your $1000 and that offers the lowest sales and purchase charges—i.e., commissions or fees.

Then what?

Do at least 10 practice trades before investing a cent. If, after ten practice trades, you still want to proceed, do so

So how do I select the stocks to buy?

That's your call. The purpose of this chapter is not to teach the successful selection and trading of stocks; millions of pages have been written on that subject.

Any other details?

A few:

● Consider a real-time quote service. The common Internet Service Providers (ISP's) like AOL provide stock quotes, *but they may lag the market*; check this out. Find a real-time service whose quotes are virtually instantaneous.

● Consider a backup ISP. If you've ever been knocked off-line during E-mail, imagine the panic when you're knocked off line while frantically trying to get out of a stock that's falling like a stone.

● Consider adjusting your attitude:

■ When a stock rises sharply during the morning and early afternoon, day traders often rush to the door as 4:00 p.m. approaches. This stampede causes an oversupply of sellers, and the stock "tanks." So, when you have a small profit, GET OUT. "You never go broke taking a profit." "I got rich trading stocks by selling too soon." (Remarks attributed to the late financier Bernard Baruch.)

■ DON'T BE AFRAID TO TAKE A LOSS. If a stock is plummeting, and little time remains, sell, sell, and SELL! He who sells and runs away will live to buy another day.

● Do not, ever, buy on margin, that is, take a loan from your broker to buy stock. Do not, ever, sell a stock ''short', that is, sell stock you don't already have. The downside risk of these maneuvers is astronomical. At least in a casino you can't lose more than your original $1000.

● Keep all records. Profits from day-trading are treated by the IRS as regular earned income—like you made from loading boxes at Bargain City last summer. For your tax return you will need to document your profits and losses. By the way, if you hold a stock for a year or more (forever to the day-trading crowd), *the tax rate on your profit falls drastically.*

Wow! Is this fun? Maybe I should forget the whole thing.

Maybe yes, maybe no. The intoxication of the market is strong. Money "won" is twice as sweet as money earned. In the end, you will learn a lot, probably lose your shirt (but hopefully not your only shirt), and emerge smarter for the long run...

9 780595 001095